⚜ The Woman's Tale

THE WOMAN'S TALE

A Journal of Inner Exploration

RONDA CHERVIN,
MARY NEILL & YOU

A Crossroad Book · *The Seabury Press* · New York

1980 / The Seabury Press
815 Second Avenue / New York, N.Y. 10017

Library of Congress Cataloging in Publication Data

Chervin, Rhonda.   The woman's tale.
"A Crossroad book."
Bibliography
    1. Women—Conduct of life.   2. Chervin, Ronda.
3. Neill, Mary.   I. Neill, Mary, joint author.
II. Title.
BJ1610.C52   158'.1   79–25024   ISBN 0-8164-2016-5

Grateful acknowledgment is made to the
following for permission to use the
poetry listed:

Sara Hyatt—"Exercising Baby."

Peggy Powell—"Links of My Life."

Alfred A. Knopf, Inc.—"The World as Meditation,"
© 1952 by Wallace Stevens, published in
The Collected Poems.

❧ Contents

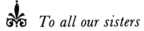 *To all our sisters*

⚜ Letter to Our Readers

The Woman's Tale was written as the fruit of an intellectual, spiritual, and emotional exchange about life and womanhood which took place between the authors during the summer session of the University of San Francisco in 1978.

Searching for a way to continue the flow over the distance between Los Angeles and San Francisco, we decided to use the symbolic feminine characters of fairytale and myth to trigger reflection on our own inner journeys. Each weekend we would write our reactions to the archetypal story personality and then send what we had written to each other for comment.

The finished version of The Woman's Tale has become a text for courses and workshops. The responses of our readers have been wonderfully rich and original as women move away from contemporary clichés into the depths of their own life-tales.

The Woman's Tale is designed to be a trialogue with your participation to accompany the reflections of the two authors. We hope you will want to share your responses with us.

We strongly suggest that as you read you keep a notebook at hand for recording your own reflections. Each chapter will include questions to spark your response.

So now we offer you our dialogue—eager to have you make it a trialogue!

Ronda Chervin and Mary Neill

Part 1

WHO AM I?

❧ Response by
Ronda Chervin

This question can be surprisingly upsetting for a woman today. Should she describe herself first in terms of her relationships to others, to her own individual self-image, or to her roles in society?

A few years ago an interviewer asked me casually how I wanted to be described, and I found myself unable to decide. Did he expect me to say wife and mother first, or professor, or writer? Would I feel guilty if I said writer first, or condemned in another way if I said wife and mother first? Do I find myself changing the description to suit the imagined views of those who ask? Sometimes, probably.

But here, in this book of exploration, we are trying to go into the depths of our own self-understanding—who am I right now as I come to you, my reader, who is unknown to me?

I am Ronda. First of all, a Catholic; a convert at twenty-one from an atheistic, though Jewish, background. My sense of identity with Christ in the church is my greatest joy, my primary source of being.

I am a woman. More and more I see myself as essentially, not accidentally, woman. From my womanhood flows being wife to my husband, Martin, a writer and consultant; and being mother to our three children: twin girls, Carla and Diana, presently sixteen, and a boy, Charles, now seven. Although the burdens con-

3

nected with family life are often exhausting, I love being a wife and mother.

I am a university professor of philosophy. I was more than half-way through my doctorate at Fordham University when I left to marry Martin. I returned to academia when the twins were a year and a half. My thesis was on the Danish philosopher-theologian Sören Kierkegaard. Though I planned to do no more than part-time teaching while bringing up what I hoped would become a family of thirteen children, a series of miscarriages and my husband's disabling illness led me into full-time teaching at Loyola Marymount University of Los Angeles. Here I specialize in Christian personalism and enjoy devising course structures to facilitate the transition from classroom to community, from abstract reasoning to personal integration.

I am a prolific writer. My first books were written for my students. *The Church of Love* was created to show Catholics the powerful affective significance of doctrines they thought of as dead letters. *The Art of Choosing* is a workbook for self-confrontation about life-styles. *Prayer and Your Everyday Life, The Spirit and Your Everyday Life,* and *Love and Your Everyday Life* were written for a mother's group to show how spirituality can become part of our moment by moment consciousness. *The Way, the Truth, and the Life* is a booklet designed to meet the need for a simple introduction to Christian prayer with individual and group exercises. *Why I am a Charismatic,* the latest work to be published, is my defense of the emotions as intrinsic to the spiritual life. Forthcoming is *Christian Ethics in Your Everyday Life*—with a workbook format. .

I realize that to many women I represent a sort of ideal combination of roles and achievements. Lecturing extensively to women's groups and meeting questions like "How do you do it all?" I find myself responding sometimes with a laugh, but often with a sigh: "I don't combine all these things well. I do them all rather badly." Or, "You are imagining the delights of each of these roles; if you had to live one hour with the amassed tensions of these jobs, you wouldn't envy me!"

As you will see from the chapters to follow the struggle to harmonize commitment and individual fulfillment unites all women.

What Do I Love About Being a Woman?

I cannot remember ever wishing to be a man instead of a woman, except perhaps as a child reading *The Black Stallion* and thinking it doubtful a girl could have played the lead.

Growing up in a female-dominated household—with a strong feminist mother, and a father who left us when my twin sister and I were eight—I thought of women as being superior rather than inferior. Women could do everything men could do and carry babies as well.

Women to me meant warmth and comfort and companionship. Men were strangers, people who left you unexpectedly, never to return; people who cared more about teaching you things and providing materially for you than holding you when you were crying or giggling with you at play.

I am sure that what I love most about being a woman is the emotional richness and freedom I experience as feminine. Of course, I have known many warm, fatherly men. I even realize now in later life how much love my own father had for me as a child. But most men I view as trapped by false values—thinking that qualities such as success, freedom, strength could be more valuable than love!

As a woman, I feel justified, so to speak, in being as emotional as I want, in loving passionately, weeping in pain, manifesting delight through affection and exuberance, flowing lyrically in response to beauty, loving God in a direct heart-to-heart communion.

I love being a woman teacher—being personal in class, motherly to my students, sometimes being funny and coy. I love being a woman writer, developing what Pascal called the *logique du coeur* instead of cold reasoning.

I love having a creative center within my physical body, a warm cavern to house new creatures, breasts from which a pure nourishing substance can flow to feed my babies. Though not as central, it is also part of my sense of being a woman to be able to leave my hair long and loose and to wear flowing dresses.

These ways of loving being a woman have grown with the

years. I can remember as a teenager valuing success more than love. I used to study all day in college, relegating friendship and love to coffee breaks and Saturday night. Proving myself equal or superior to men in teaching sometimes would overshadow the desire to love and be loved.

The older I get, now forty-one, the more I value what I think of as typically feminine emotions. The joy of some external success or swift razor-sharp refutation of an opponent is quickly quenched by the knowledge that I have failed in loving or alienated love others might have given.

What Do I Hate About Being a Woman?

I hate being so much at the mercy of my emotions. A somewhat volatile type, I go up and down on roller coasters of intense moods of elation and despair. Although I would not sacrifice the excitement of these passions for some sterile calm, I long desperately for fewer mood swings, for an ability which I see more often in men than in women to bring emotions under the control of the will or the intellect.

I hate having to do petty tasks such as clearing the table, changing a diaper, cleaning house at the very times when I am at a peak of creative work or stimulating conversation. To see men continuing a discussion while I am exiled to the kitchen irritates me to death. I do not mind the same chores so much when only women are around, for we follow each other, offering help amidst our rounds, instead of taking exemptions from common tasks.

I hate the difficulty I find in governing my chattering tongue. It seems that I have to express myself no matter how inappropriate or even harmful it is to my own goals. I envy the solemn silences of wise men and even the shrewd silences of talkative men when it suits their strategy.

The House I Live in Now

I live in a large, bright green, modern stucco house in Los Angeles. My husband does the decorating. He loves to accumulate pictures, photos, lamps, mobiles, hanging plants, and so on. The house is full of life. It has a small, somewhat neglected garden and a yard. Upstairs my husband has built a music-listening and writing room for himself. He writes in the mornings and listens to music in the evenings—I join him sometimes and sit and comment on student papers. Knitting is my hobby, and the house is full of personalized afghans and blankets. Just recently, I took possession of a room to use as a study—previously, I did all my work stretched out on our large bed. I spend long hours now in the study, which also serves as a prayer room, with a prie-dieu and my favorite religious paintings.

Previously unkempt and rather dirty, the house has changed considerably since I finally gave in and decided to get a once-a-week helper to clean. This has greatly lessened the tensions caused by my trying to get other members of the family to clean up so that I would not have to.

My interior house? The inside of me I would liken to a battlefield of conflicting forces—rage, hope, fear, longing, delight, frustration, disappointment, excitement, love, and even occasionally, deep peace. I think of my inside house as being rather messy, and yet I know that there is much beauty there, along with great forces for goodness and love. Some rare times I have lived inside a harmonized me, and I know it is possible and poignantly beautiful.

What Window Do I Look Out Of?
During daily Mass or prayer times, I look out of the stained-glass window of faith, hope, and love, and the world seems lovely—even the ugly and painful seem as the wounds of Christ. During times of busyness or fatigue or frustration, I look out the smudgy, moldy cellar windows of my soul's house and I see everything as hopeless and disgusting—a world abandoned by a God who gave up. I see things as Sartre's characters do in his most cynical novels and plays.

What Do I Hope For From This Book?
To love myself more as I am. I have hope that the tangled knot of my conflicting emotions will move toward a coherent tale. To choose the paths of hope revealed through self-confrontation instead of being mired in the quicksand of my own fears. To be able

to love my dear family with the patience coming from deep confidence in the meaning of life. To love people less suspiciously or defensively or possessively, because I understand their differences and accept mine. To become a wiser mentor of my students from savoring their tales.

⚜ Response by Mary Neill

I am forty-five years old, a Dominican Sister since 1950, a teacher since 1955. I received my doctorate after studying theology in France.

Presently I teach Religious Studies at the University of San Francisco, largely to undergraduates. I give journal workshops, run a dream group for women and regularly offer brief courses at Marin Junior College for its Adult Education Program.

I was raised in the South until I was eleven, but have spent most of my life in northern California. My father and mother are still alive, and I have a married older sister.

Why do I want to write a book for women at this time when the market seems to be teeming with such books—often, to me, half-thought-out, half-well-wrought notions of feminine consciousness? Selfishly, I want to articulate my viewpoint, which I but rarely find represented—and in looking at my concepts, help their growth in form and substance.

A brief review of my response to the leading magazines for women will introduce you to my reasons for seeking an alternate vision.

Ladies' Home Journal and other magazines of the same type seem to assume that my central concerns might be recipes, skin care, diet control, sexual response, home decoration and fashion.

Ms. assures me that my greater freedom lies in the direction of the passage of ERA, the easy availability of abortion for all (my body belongs to me!), and the revamping of language by feminist fiat, so that justice may be furthered when I address chairpersons, spokespersons, and fisherpersons. (How I wish sometimes it were so, that I could reshape reality by reshaping my language rather than struggling with the shape that language has given me, struggle even just for my own style and pronunciation.)

I subscribe to *Ms.* though I am frequently bored by its lack of nuance, occasionally enraged by its vulgarity and infrequently impressed by a deeply written article. Why? Because it seems to mirror that triad in all of us of banality, vulgarity, and depth. Most of all because it takes women seriously. It is human somehow in its lopsidedness and intensity, even if sad in its counterdependence on all that is traditional—the new wave must be better; the inherent law of utopia. The new wave is often just new dogma; although it suspects all old dogmas. Both the hopes and despairs of *Ms.* strike me as unbalanced and immoderate.

And what does writing this book mean to me as a woman of faith? To believe in God and trust totally in him alone and only partially in things created is to admit that we are not God, allknowing, all-powerful, unlimited. Rather, we are limited, dependent, mortal, human. Even the antireligious Sigmund Freud said that the human being's desire to be God is a central problem in growing to mature relations.

Does admitting dependence on God as central mean accepting all other dependencies causing bitter frustration in a woman's life? Should we acquiesce in the old definition of woman as one who is dependent, who must wait and watch, who must take care, who must please? Is woman forever to be one who serves others, who encompasses, makes peace, understands? Woman, the *yin,* the passive, dark receptive waters waiting to be animated by *yang,* the male, the light, the active. Her fullness, she is told, is in receiving, complementing, yielding.

According to this vision, woman is one who awaits the strong opposite to create new life out of her chaos of uncertainty, vulnerability, fallibility, incompleteness. Woman is haunted by the *more;* she hungers, at times, to be swept away, to be transformed by another.

Woman, as mother, receives life, nurtures it from her own being, then gives away that life to its own directions and autonomies. "Did you not know that I must be about my Father's business?" That question Jesus asked Mary is asked in some form by every child who leaves. The mother is left to ponder an emptiness that was once filled, but now again is vacuum.

So we find woman caring for life and letting it go. If man has a mountain to climb, woman's mountain often seems to be man— the elusive other. Outside of relating to another, complementing another's life task, she often feels incomplete in a way that a man seems not to.

Moreover, she often enjoys profound satisfaction in entering deeply into another person's world, becoming a central part of the other's landscape. She loves to adorn another's life, to crown it with joy and gladness. She adorns her body for her beloved perhaps in part as a symbol of her adorning of the other's life. She attracts, cajoles, seduces, charms, wins, enchants, hovers, orbits, enhances, serves. Women is she who is dependent.

But if she is honest, there will come moments (to be trusted somehow) when she hates all this—despises her dependency, caring little whether it comes, as some say, from the nature of her body with its concave receptacles tied to a twenty-eight-day lunar tide or whether it comes from false psychological categories and societal roles. Wherever this dependency comes from, there comes a time when almost every woman hates it as her bane and her destiny—hates that she is not enough by herself, that there is a force within her, driving her to give herself away to another who will complete and save and redeem her, giving her new life.

Some women, perhaps in the worst kind of despair, never bring this hatred of dependency to consciousness; instead they cop out by hating their husbands and children, or their religious congregation, or whoever they can blame for their discomfort. They have given their all for completeness and it was not enough. The sense of fulfillment was momentary, and they suspect they have sold their soul for a mess of potage. Acting easily and instinctively, they shouldered their dependent roles, only to feel betrayed by their generosity: they feel cheated, "had," burned, used.

To confront, to question, to embrace one's dependency as coming from within; to explore what makes us want to give ourselves away; to try to sort out what is to be trusted in our dependency, what is to be challenged—this is the task of an inward exploration, of a hard spiritual journey to the underworld.

Woe to the woman whose passions, indignation, hate, despair is not strong enough to plunge her into the journey, so that she may arrive with hope at the other shore. The woman afraid to feel her anger, her limitations, to the full, seems often doomed to fritter them away in petty bickering and negativity, or, I suggest, in peripheral political action.

In the light of this summary of some of my concerns, you can more easily understand why I find so much of Women's Liberation to be superficial with its trust in political solutions to what are sometimes deepest questions of identity.

Of course, it is simply easier and superficially more rewarding in the short run to agitate against "the others" rather than to work within. Nicholas Berdyaev noted, I know not where, that there are only two possible ways of attacking a problem: the way of the commissar, who forces others, or the yogi, who looks within, to the source of life within, to the demons within, to the death and chaos within.

The vision I trust is ultimately a religious one, that of the yogi. I guess I distrust most in the Women's Liberation Movement what I distrust in myself—the tendency to rearrange furniture instead of sticking to the task of the hard journey within where one passes through fire to come out a strong self, fully alive, no longer afraid to let oneself be used by structures, roles, and functions, because one has gotten in touch with a self that cannot be enchained.

It is easy, D. H. Lawrence noted, to run to the West, shouting of freedom and rattling one's chains; far easier than the slow, dull heave of persevering interiority. *Ms.* seems to me to do a lot of chain-rattling.

On the other hand, what I distrust in the women's nonliberation movement, in the stance articulated by *Total Woman* or by women's magazines such as the *Journal,* is that there is no journey, no movement. Though I don't subscribe to these magazines, I browse through them regularly and pleasantly spend an hour there—never rattled, as by *Ms.,* but never surprised, either. This spring I read an issue of the *Journal* that was printed five years ago and became suspicious of its date only when the stories on Jackie Onassis and Liz Taylor were accompanied by tattletale, too-young-looking pictures. Glamour is glamour is glamour. And outer ornamentation is easier than inner.

In this sense, *Ms.* and *Journal* are (under the skin) amazingly alike in their approach—shouting "freedom" louder and making things look better. I search for inner bones that will help me walk upright and I find lots of remedies. This is perhaps more unfair to *Ms.* than *Journal.*

When, as a religious Sister, I turn to religious periodicals to help clarify how these dry bones shall live, I experience the same sense of not being the person they are addressing. *Sisters Today* leaves me remembering a poem or a quotation from its cover, never its content. *Review for Religious* convinces me somehow that I would fail for the test for which it seems to be reviewing—I know I will not have the proper attitude toward the new canon law, the discussions on masturbation, or the latest Biblical criticism.

So, since nothing I read directed to women in general or religious in particular fits me, I thought I would try to suit myself and anyone else out there who feels alienated by the world vision of *Ms.*, bored with the complacency of ladies' magazines—someone neither *Total Woman* or Gloria Steinem, neither liberal nor conservative, yet some of both.

Someone like me living her own story of life and death as faithfully and truthfully as she can, colored, bonded, in all the physical and cultural roots she moves perseveringly within; committing herself to love freely all that she has come from and all that she is being called to become by God and by all the others whom he sends into her life. She who lives with both radical dependence and resolute aloneness, seeing the inevitability and the gift of both. Anyone out there like me?

What Do I Like About Being a Woman?

There have come certain moments of oneness which I have felt when swimming in the sea, or lying on the earth—a kind of safety within sacredness; a sureness that whatever comes in my life and passes away, some nurture, some love, some life remains within and without in a silence known by the sea and the land. I have been comforted in homesickness lying on the ground under a tree in the Rhine forest; I have listened to the sea and felt a peace, knowing that I have both a profound emptiness, and yet a fertile soil within me; when flood tides, a rhythm that will ebb and flow. There's a sureness I feel about the larger life questions that comes, I sense, from being a woman.

I do not mean to imply that all women feel this way; I only speak of what these moments of identity have meant for me. And, yes, I have stood in the burnt-out hollow of a thousand-year-old redwood tree and felt its strength and age surround me, and known surely some "woman" thing about the tree and me. The tree is mother and has endured the eating out of its heart through inner fire. I shall endure the fire and find shelter, and I shall give it.

I have read men poets who felt this oneness, this movement with the earth and sea. Yet in their poetry, I never felt they loved the earth and sea as the SAME, but as OTHER. I am sea and soil, rock and tree. I am woman. I have never wanted to be a man, nor imagined that I could be, though for twenty years I carried a man's name, that of Matthias, the belated disciple. When friends ask why I changed back to Mary, I answer, "I never made it as a man." Maybe I'll never make it as a woman either, but I'm glad I'm a woman, even if my "woman" feelings are maybe too englobalizing, cosmic, or mystic.

My first deep self-consciousness came when I was about four years old, playing dolls on a rock under a pine tree in the Colorado mountains. If that colored my woman consciousness "nature-cosmic," so be it. What is the color of your consciousness? When did it come? At what moments do you know that you are a woman and are glad?

What Do I Dislike About Being a Woman?

That it matters so much what I look like doesn't seem fair; that I have more cultural directives than do men to worry about body shape and clothes and hair and attractiveness. (The *Journal* sells because of these strong, seemingly unchanging directives.) Erich Fromm thinks that physical attractiveness is more important for women because man's sexual response can fail—it needs to be triggered in a way that woman's of necessity need not. Simply, a woman can love an ugly man; the reversal is far more difficult and many women suffer from it.

Every woman seems to need inwardly to have someone see and name her as beautiful. Cultural norms make this naming hard, chancy, and arbitrary. In China, a woman must have beautiful feet; in Japan, a lovely neck; in Africa, a generous *derrière;* in the United States, a glamorous bust. It seems ridiculous and cruel— and irrevocably mandated.

I remember once when teaching high school being "middle-woman," arranging dates for a junior prom. Once, when asked if the girl I was "procuring" as his date was good-looking, I assured the lad that "She's as good-looking a girl as you are a boy." "That's not enough," he said. And that was that. Even as a nun, when by commitment, I have removed myself from the courting market, it still matters too much to too many people if I'm marketably attractive. When I shave my legs, tweeze my whiskers, worry over a run in my stockings, decide for or against a girdle, I do so because as a woman I've got to look better than my male counterpart. And I don't like it.

And I don't like it that John Wayne and Cary Grant played romantic leads well into their sixties while Joan Fontaine and Bette Davis could only become "character" actresses, never objects of romance after forty. Lovable women are young and pretty. Two very beautiful women I know have suffered much from their beauty because they were not, could not be sure of whether they were loved inwardly. Nobody wins.

I dislike, too, that I can never join the men's club that controls so much of American life. No amount of work, skill, savvy will give me the passport, the credentials that a male has from his very body. I am much more sympathetic to men than I used to be— they pay a high price to belong to that club; I see they resent, and rightly, some women's expectation that they should belong to this club without paying their dues. But what if you pay your dues, and you still can't belong? It isn't fair.

As I look over my spontaneous answers, I notice that both what I like and dislike deal with body experiences. My "likes" seem to my inner critic too "large" a "plus" to be taken seriously; my complaints seem too small, too petty. But, like Goldilocks, I am willing on this journey to try the chairs that are too big or too small; the soup that is too hot or too cold, until I find that bed which is "just right." Until we write down honestly our prejudices, it is hard to move them on. What are your prejudices about books and magazines written for women? What book would you write? Can you own the *Ms.* (the Gloria Steinem) in you? and the *Ladies' Home Journal* addict? Can you love them both and not be encapsuled in their expectations of what a woman should be?

What are your great expectations for women? If *Ms.* has too utopian expectations and the *Journal* is too flimsy, what is "just right"? Are you afraid to dialogue with the "hot" and the "cold" of it? Why? Do you cling to an unexamined middle position? To an unexamined life?

What Is the Home I Live In?
My home is not a home, or even a convent really. It is a large four-story San Francisco Victorian academy built in 1906, just in time for the great fire and earthquake. It survived well and still draws a large number of young women from the suburbs.

It is a hard building to make into a home, as are all institutions. But we fifteen nuns who live on the edges of the building enjoy its age and charm, despite its inconveniences (it has no center room, institutions don't seem to have "hearth" places), and I must walk up eighty-four stairs to get to my fourth-floor dormer room. To be married to the church, as it were, is to live in strange buildings like this—to wonder at their survival and their relevance to this time and age.

But the school, built in the heart of the city, smack on the edge of the ghetto on one side and elegant Pacific Heights on the other, survives, and so do we nuns. Something of an anachronism, perhaps, and a living question mark.

It is a house on the margin, an institution on the margin, which speaks to me of my own marginality, my own personal call to be a Dominican, a monk, a person Thomas Merton defines this way: "He struggles with the fact of death, trying to seek something deeper than death, and the office of the monk or the marginal person, the meditative person or the poet, is to go beyond death even in this life, to go beyond the dichotomy of life and death and be, therefore, a witness to life."[1]

What Do I See Out of My Window?

In my small room, I have one high dormer window from which I can see the sky and a few rooftops. I must stand on a stool to look down at the street below. Perhaps this, too, is part of what being a religious is—having a room of your own; Virginia Woolf's *A Room of One's Own* underlines its importance for self-growth. Privacy and a place to grow, to pray, to sort out the world. Do you have an inner or outer room of your own?

My window reminds me of what may be a hazardous aspect of religious life; we are protected from life on the streets—the life that most people live. I can easily live in my ivory tower here and I must stretch to gaze into that world sometimes. Too often my temptation is to gaze skyward to rooftops and block out street scenes. My life call is to a kind of skywardness, to sublimation ("Our Father, who art in heaven"), but so it is also to earthwardness ("And the word was made flesh"—he came down from heaven and was made man). I must work to become woman, the one woman I am in this one flesh that was given to me.

My room at work—my office—has no window—this man's world that is the University of San Francisco. Not having a window is hard, and I have often made harsh feminist judgments about the masculine consciousness that could build rooms without windows. But when I was given an opportunity to move from the room, I found I had grown attached to it; I had learned to create inner windows where there were none outside. The dark room reminds me of the dark, windowless rooms within me that the Lord patiently gives me grace and grit to illuminate; of the fresh air inner freedom must bring to locked, dark places. And what has been freely given to me, I am called to give freely; to help students create inner windows where there are none given outside.

Your Turn

Now you, as our reader, may want to write an introduction to your own life-tale using your notebook. Write free style or, if you prefer, frame your answers to some of the same questions we asked ourselves: Who am I? What do I love about being a woman? About myself as a woman? What do I hate about being a woman? About myself as a woman? What house do I live in? What windows do I look out of? What do I hope for from working with this book?

Part 2

SPINNING OFF OF TWICE-TOLD TALES

We turn now to the part of The Woman's Tale *devoted to pondering the symbolic girls and women of the fairytales as a path of inner-exploration.*

Depending on time and inclination, you may choose to read and respond to all the chapters and questions or pick out from the collection those you immediately identify with, checking out the list on the contents' page.

Some of the fairytales you probably know from childhood from constant repetition in books, TV, or movies. Others may be fairly new, at least in the versions we've selected. For this reason, each chapter will begin with a short summary of the fairytale.

After reading our reflections, write your own response to the tale as it illuminates your life, rounding out your exploration with illustrations, poems, or sayings and also jotting down any ideas coming out of sharing if you are in a group. Spin away!

⚜ Snow-White and Rose-Red
Sisterhood is Powerful

S now-White and Rose-Red are sisters. Snow-White, quiet and gentle, helps their widowed mother keep house; Rose-Red runs and jumps about in the meadows, gathering flowers and catching butterflies.

The two children love each other so dearly that they always walk hand in hand when they go out together. And when Snow-White says, "We will never separate from each other," Rose-Red replies, "Not so long as we live!" And their mother says, "What each girl has, she must share with the other."

No beast harms them and the good angel guards them if they sleep through the night in the forest. In the evenings, a lamb and a dove are by their side as they listen to their mother read from the Great Book.

One snowy evening Rose-Red opens the door to the knock of a great black bear. Snow-White hides. Their mother tells them not to be afraid of the bear.

Through the winter they play with the bear, but in the summer he leaves them to return and guard his treasures from evil dwarfs. For "what has once passed into dwarfs' hands and is hidden by them in caves is not easily brought to light." As the bear leaves, it is Snow-White who glimpses gold through a hole in his hairy coat.

The two girls in their journeys, never far from home, meet the evil dwarf three times—first caught in a tree, then by a fish, and then by an eagle. In helping him, Snow-White keeps snipping off bits of his beard with the scissors she keeps in her pocket.

The dwarf is always irritable, rude, and ungrateful for the help of the girls. When they come upon him emptying his bag of precious stones, he starts to abuse them until a great black bear comes who kills him with one blow. As the frightened girls run away, the bear calls them back and stands revealed to them as a prince in gold cloth: a king's son now released from the wicked dwarf's curse.

Snow-White marries the prince and Rose-Red marries his brother, and they live happily with their mother in a palace with the dwarf's immense treasure. In front of the palace grow the red and white rose bushes that once adorned their cottage.

So satisfying is this tale to me, so well constructed in its symbolism, that it is hard to start to pull it apart. I am nourished by the unity of the sisters, never apart in their beginnings, their adventures, their endings. They are never pulled apart. They never work against one another, though they are different in coloring and disposition. This story pulls at me, threads its way through my own story because I grew up with a sister who seemed Rose-Red to my Snow-White, going our very different life ways, finding it hard to share each other's lives.

Perhaps more poignantly, my *inner* sisters, my gentle, contemplative aspects, and my red roving spirit have not always lived as good sisters to one another. So much of my inner (and outer) conflicts have stumbled around this white/red dichotomy. And, too often, the inner mother of my mind favors one over the other.

For instance, at this time in my life I get disproportionately annoyed at my chronic "good girl" aspects, the mother's girl who shines copper kettles and carries scissors in her pocket. My Rose-Red says, mockingly at times: "You fearful establishment baby, clinging to safe cottages, afraid to run and risk. I wish you'd change and not be so careful, so afraid of what comes knocking at your door."

At other times, my Snow-White scolds, "Rose-Red, you wild and restless butterfly, never settling in, don't you know that bears are dangerous?"

Too often in my life I have mistakenly seen Snow-White as my spiritual side; Rose-Red as trouble-making and demonic. The long hold of Manicheanism in Western consciousness, with its god of light vs. god of darkness dualism, that evolved into Catharism in the twelfth century and Jansenism in the seventeenth century, have their hold on me, not just conceptually, but experientially.

I see part of my vocation to the Dominican order as a search for a healing of this dualism. Dominic, who founded his order to fight the flesh-hating Cathari, insisted that Dominicans not choose between black and white (but wear them both); not choose between cloister and world (but live in them both) nor between action and contemplation. Our motto, *Contemplata aliis tradere* (to give to others the fruit of one's contemplation) is a snow-white, rose-red one. Our shield, insignia *Veritas,* "Truth," refers to the truth that is Christ, the God-Man in whom all opposites have their healing, their union.

But this immersement in the truth, this mind dyeing with Christ's consciousness ("I would have you in you that mind which was in Christ Jesus," says Paul to the Philippians) is not easily come by on an emotional level.

Seeking healing of the dualism between Snow-White and Rose-Red means journeying out of carefully kept cottages into the wilds; it means encounters with dwarfed parts of us. It means learning from what seems inferior to us—the bear, the fish, the eagle, the lamb, and the dove. How often have I experienced a stunted, irritable, ungrateful, abusive part of me that has cursed my princely nature, buried immense treasures of energy and love in dark caves "most inaccessible to light."

The fairytale also raises this perennial dilemma of femininity: how can virginal innocents, raised to shopping for thread, needles, pins, laces, and ribbons (as the tale says)—so vulnerable—successfully encounter the journey-dangers of theft, killing, enslavement? The story gives clues to solving this moral conundrum which ultimately puzzles everyone's life. How can that which is weak and vulnerable prevail against profound dangers, inner and outer?

Primarily, the fairytale teaches this truth: by not trying to make it alone; by *sharing:* "What belongs to one, belongs to the other." Outwardly the sharing of one's gifts brings great strength inwardly. And within, sharing means owning—admitting to—and living with one's contraries, one's opposites, one's shadow, parts that are ours "so long as we live."

Too often, we would clean up the ambiguity in our personalities by giving death decrees to difficult aspects of ourselves; then we walk about a living lie, often projecting what we have rejected onto others. We share inwardly also by honoring our instinctual life as well as our symbolic life; in our single body are all the opposites made one (as in Christ's single body are many made one).

We honor oneness and sharing by creating a nurturing consciousness (and this calls for right-mindfulness and patient self-examination), a good mothering inner-home, a home that loves both red and white, war and peace, life and death.

We must relentlessly rid ourselves of the wicked stepmother in each of us which would demean, dishonor, orphan certain aspects of ourselves as awkward, unseasonal, untimely. We need all our qualities to remain flexible in our journey, pliable to life's turnings; to honor all the seasons in our lives. It is when we honor the powerful sisterhood within us, the Snow-White and the Rose-Red, that we can live with the deep peace resonating in this passage from Ecclesiastes:

> There is an appointed time for everything and a time for every affair under heaven.
> A time to be born and a time to die; a time to plant and a time to uproot the plant.
> A time to kill and a time to heal; a time to tear down and a time to build.
> A time to weep and a time to laugh; a time to mourn and a time to dance.
> A time to scatter stones and a time to gather them; a time to embrace and a time to be far from embraces.
> A time to seek and a time to lose; a time to keep and a time to cast away.
> A time to tear and a time to sew; a time to be silent and a time to speak.
> A time to love and a time to hate; a time of war and a time of peace . . . I have considered the task which God has appointed for me to be busied about. He has made every-

thing appropriate to its time and has put the timeless into their hearts, without men's ever discovering from beginning to end, the work which God has done (Eccles. 3:1–12).

At one time, meeting a woman but briefly on a weekend and being very attracted to her, I saw that she represented a lost sister. Writing a poem (which I quote in part) clarified the soul-hunger that attractions often illuminate:

> *Then shall my heart leap from out your fingertips*
> *To run for joy!*
> *That sisters light and dark, Snow-White/Rose-Red*
> *Do in one flesh, one heart*
> *Each to each, each in each*
> *Hold dogged death and separation, loss and crippled laming*
> *For a hunter's breath, at bay—*
> *While Eden flashes in that moment:*
> *Paradise where Adam walks at eventide with God*
> *Calling all the animals by their true and separate name in Christ-to-come,*
> *And Eva, Ave, ever Maria*
> *Holds all her strange and varied children*
> *Yet peaceful one in her warm womb.*

Having read this explication of Snow-White and Rose-Red, write your own responses in the space below. This may be done either free style or by answering some of the following questions:

1. Do you see yourself as more like the quiet gentle Snow-White or more like the adventuresome Rose-Red? Give examples of these qualities in yourself and possibly in your sisters, girl friends, or woman friends. Do you think that women in general have been trained to have more Snow-White in them or more Rose-Red?

2. In Mary Neill's response you will see that she thinks of Snow-White and Rose-Red as symbolizing two parts of her one self-hood. In the fairytale, the mother wants Snow-White and Rose-Red to be always together. As we "mother" ourselves, we should let the gentle and the adventuresome complement each

other. Do you see these qualities in yourself as at war or together in peace?

3. Why does Snow-White get the bear-prince as husband, though Rose-Red was the first to open the door? Relate this question to your own life and your image of woman.

4. Do different men friends and women friends bring to life the Snow-White or the Rose-Red in you, or both?

Response to Snow-White and Rose-Red

RONDA CHERVIN

Mary's reflection had a great impact on me. At first it seemed to me that there was no Snow-White in me at all. But this is not so. I love to sit quietly and knit. Studying is also a form of being Snow-White—reading, thinking, listening. I love an orderly schedule with definite things planned for each time. I hate change in the external sphere.

For a happy family life, it is essential that the Snow-White element be strong. Often adventurous single people cannot bear the commitment to routine that family life entails. If they get married on impulse, they soon leave. On the other hand, too much Snow-White becomes monotonous and leads even the most domestic of women into fantasies of escape. It seems that part of the secret of a happy life is to "expect the unexpected," as Heraclitus said, in the form of allowing for new challenges and experiences within the framework of an orderly existence. As in the story, it is Rose-Red who opens the door to the bear, but it is Snow-White who sees the gold and knows how to bring lasting treasure out of adventure.

I am intrigued by Mary's idea of the inner mother of your mind favoring one sister over the other illegitimately. I think a good question would be to ask which girl each of our own mothers favored. In my case, I view my mother as favoring Rose-Red, but at the same time sending out the confusing signal that you have to be Snow-White to fit into the household rhythms. I resented being told I had to be Snow-White after glorious images of the delights of being Rose-Red, the adventurous one, had been depicted to me in seductive colors.

The inner mother of my own mind seems always to scold—she scolds Rose-Red for being too free and Snow-White for being content with trivia. My inner mother blesses neither Rose-Red nor Snow-White but instead plays them off against one another. No wonder I am so tense!

I also resent anyone who blesses one of the "sisters" to the exclusion of the other. For example, I resent being told to be Snow-White in family life—"just do your little chores peacefully." I become almost claustrophobic if surrounded by Snow-White domestic women without wings. Ultra-neat, modest, sedate women, whether they be wives, singles, or nuns, make me want to do something outrageous to shock and perhaps throttle them into life.

But when I let Rose-Red have full sway to the exclusion of Snow-White, or meet someone else who does, or even read about such women, I feel threatened by such terrifying abysses that I decide to give Rose-Red a death sentence, as Mary so graphically put it. When I have cut off Rose-Red's head, I fall gratefully into the arms of Snow-White, but with poor results. For example, while working on this piece, I decided on a self-devised moral improvement program for restraining the impulsiveness of Rose-Red. Three days into the routine I was so miserable I was for killing everything in sight, myself especially.

Mary's reflections about Rose-Red and Snow-White suggest strongly that such attempts to guillotine or scold one or the other of the sisters will not work. Instead we should seek harmony—perhaps by means of allowing different times for each to shine? Let one go out wandering, then sit quietly and contemplate, then give, then seek again?

The idea of accepting both and reconciling the opposites is challenging to me, yet seemingly unattainable. In fact, the thought of such a demand for harmony makes me feel even more inclined to opt for one or the other sister, either/or, burning all bridges behind me, either to live intensely for the moment with no restraints or to hide in a corner and knit, cutting out my tongue lest it offend God and man.

And yet I do know moments of perfect harmony. In my writing, "the sisters" work together. I begin with ripe red adventuresome ideas or quiet butterfly images, then I sit quietly and knit these opposites into the whole of a well-ordered book.

And most of all, when I am deep in prayer, I experience God blessing each of the sisters separately and together. Did He not bless with sanctity such opposites as Teresa of Avila, the fiery saint of Spain, and Thérèse of Lisieux, the domestic contemplative of the little way? I chose both of these saints as my patrons. Was I hoping to make them friends?

Turning to another of Mary Neill's fruitful images: "We have to encounter the dwarf within . . . the stunted, irritable, ungrateful, abusive part of the self, cursing our princely nature."

I recognize this description of the dwarf as characteristic of women both at home and at work. In family life, this shrewishness may be so blatant it requires no probing to bring to light. But at work it takes more subtle forms. I think that many women are like myself in the hope of transforming work situations into cozy communities. When this dream is thwarted, as will usually be the case, we become gossipy, spiteful, vengeful. I find myself making scapegoats of distant administrative figures who cannot retaliate; and ridiculing behind their backs those near at hand who could hurt me if I engaged them in open battle.

Such dwarflike behavior can lead to getting caught in the brambles. Eventually we must resort to Snow-White's scissors to bring us out of such states with the least possible damage to ourselves. Then we can seek constructive solutions to daily work problems. Occasionally it is to Rose-Red we must turn to lead us out to dance away singing our own songs.

The quotations from Ecclesiastes about the flow of time—a time for peace and a time for war—always disturbs rather than soothes me.

When I am letting my inner masculine hold sway, I rebel against time with a Luciferlike pride. I refuse the ebb and flow of time. I want to have all at once, all or nothing, the absolute, no finitude, no change, no growth, no development, no freedom!

In more feminine moods I express my hatred of time and imperfection by escaping into fantasies of perfect joy.

Mary's remedy is highly suggestive and challenging—to pursue possible dreams (Rose-Red) and knit them into reality (Snow-White).

I see the figure of the Virgin Mary emerging beautifully as a fulfillment of the image: Mary, mother of longing, dreaming of the Messiah, emptying herself in her yearning eros for God and receiving of the divine fullness ... then living day by day in cleaning a carpenter's house.

What aspects do different friends bring to life in me? I find that as a married woman with children and a career I seem to need friends who bring out each of the sisters. Usually neighborhood women I meet in the playground help me to do my Snow-White maypole dance more gracefully as we help each other admit to the knots and to patch up torn streamers. On the other hand I also seek someone to awaken Rose-Red lest I grow too bored. But those people who love adventure have a hard time being a friend to me since I am ever ready to reject them if they try to lead me too far out.

I loved the final poem with its image of Eve-Mary holding "all her strange and varied children peacefully in her warm womb." I feel that way when I pray the rosary. Praying it alone is like being stroked after many tears by a loving mother. Praying it with the parish ladies after Mass is like a family group in the evening with Mother looking up from time to time and smiling at each child, enjoying the Snow-Whites and the Rose-Reds, never really separate, always sharing.

You might want to crystallize your reflections by writing a poem to your lost sister, within or without, with whom you need to share your journey's trials in order to form a powerful sisterhood. Or perhaps you might quote some passage that comes to mind from other readings or draw or append a picture.

⚜ The Red Shoes

RONDA CHERVIN

The story begins with an orphan, Karen, very poor, who goes barefoot in summer and has to wear heavy wooden shoes in winter. Karen is adopted by a rich old lady. When it comes time for her confirmation, she is sent to a fashionable shoemaker to be fitted. Instead of choosing the customary black shoes, she picks out a beautiful pair of red leather shoes, just like the ones she had once seen on the feet of a princess.

During the ceremony of confirmation, Karen is so entranced by her new red shoes that she cannot concentrate on God at all. The congregation is scandalized and upbraids the old lady for letting the young girl wear such inappropriate attire. As a result, Karen is forbidden to wear any but black shoes to church.

The next Sunday Karen gives into temptation and puts on the red shoes. In front of the church door she meets an old soldier with a long beard. He asks to dust her shoes and says, "My! what beautiful dancing shoes." Clapping the soles with his hand, he adds, "Stick on tightly when you dance."

Again she is totally distracted from the church service by her love of the shoes. Once outside, the shoes force her to dance, whether she wills it or not.

Home again, the shoes are put away in a cupboard, but Karen cannot resist frequently looking in at them. Soon afterward the old lady, to whom she owes everything, becomes very sick. Karen is supposed to take care of her. But a big ball is being given, and Karen puts on the red shoes, thinking there can be no harm in this—and soon finds herself abandoning the old lady and rushing to the ball. At the dance, she finds that she cannot control the direction of her feet. She dances in a frenzy, finally outside the ballroom and into the forest. Here she meets the old soldier again. Filled with terror, she tries to kick off the shoes, but they are stuck to her feet.

Now she cannot rest but must dance all day and night through forest and meadow, in rain as well as sunshine, by day and by night.

Miserable, she finally goes to the executioner and begs him to chop off her feet. He does so. The shoes dance away with the little feet in them. She tries to go into the church to repent but wherever she goes, she sees the red shoes dancing in front of her.

Finally, she goes to the rectory and begs to work there as a servant, just for the joy of being with good people and doing penance. Still afraid to go to Sunday services, she spends the Sabbath praying and singing in her room. One day an angel of God comes, and by a miracle Karen sees the whole congregation right in her own room. She thanks God for His mercy. "The music of the organ pealed forth, and the voices of the children's choir rang out in mellow and lovely tones. The bright rays of the sun streamed warmly through the window to the pew where Karen sat. Her heart was so filled with the sunshine of peace and joy that it broke, and the sunbeams carried her soul to heaven. No one there questioned her about the red shoes."

Such is the original story by Hans Christian Andersen. In the movie of the same title, we see the fairytale as a ballet, with Moira Shearer as the Karen figure. The soldier becomes an inviting but demonic shoemaker. The red shoes in the ballerina's own life become symbols of the dance itself as career, the pursuit of which becomes a frenzy, and takes demonic precedence over all human claims.

The heroine of the movie falls in love with a composer and marries him; she plans to put the role of wife before that of ballerina. At the climax, she is supposed to attend the debut of a new composition by her husband. But at the last moment she rushes away to play her lead in the ballet of the Red Shoes.

In her dressing room Karen is following the radio broadcast of her husband's performance. An announcement is made that the conductor will not be present. In fact, he's on his way to his wife's dressing room to beg her to leave the ballet again for good. Unable to resolve her conflict, she rushes down the many steps outside the theater overlooking a railroad track. The camera focuses on her feet, in the red ballet shoes, going faster and faster. She throws herself under an oncoming train. Next we see her blood-stained feet and her husband weeping over them, and finally the ballet performance with the shoemaker in tears, pantomiming a dance without its heroine.

The story of the Red Shoes has such a deep meaning for me that even its retelling makes me tremble.

I was first introduced to the tale through the lavish film which I saw over and over again as a teenager. In general, I think it is often revealing to see what movie or book any person views or reads over and over again. This may provide many clues to the central self-image most intoxicating and painful in each individual's life-tale.

And so, answering the following questions is no mere academic exercise for me but rather a powerful reenactment of a dance that forms a permanent part of my own life.

1. What do the red shoes represent in my life—past, present, future? In my case, there is an actual pair of red shoes. After seeing the film for the first time, I bought my sister, a dancer, a very expensive pair of red ballet shoes just like the ones in the movie. Not a ballet dancer, but of the modern school, she never wore them so they hung on the wall for years in symbolic splendor.

As a child, I used to get into manic moods and dance in a frenzy around the house. I did not like actual dance classes, however, since they were sober and involved lots of hard work. I wanted *the ecstasy without the discipline*. Perhaps in that phrase "ecstasy without discipline," I find a clue to the central problem I face in every area of life.

If I think of the red shoes as a symbol of frenzied ecstasy leading to collapse, it would describe my rhythm of creativity. I cannot begin a project for a new course at the university, or an article or book I might write, without first getting into a state of extreme delight about the idea. Riding a peak of excitement, I am driven to a swift sketching out of the task. With the red shoes still on my feet, I carry out the further steps of making the project concrete. Then tireder and tireder, I begin to wish I could get out of completing the project, and even out of life itself, which is so exhausting. But I can't quit. I bring everything to a conclusion, sink into a heap, descend into black despair, and wait for the glitter of a new spark so I may don my red shoes and set off again in a new frenzy.

The same is true in love relationships. I am entranced by the beauty of someone's personality. I begin to circle around the person in a sort of dance of delight. I accelerate the pace faster and faster. Usually, the other person withdraws from too much intensity. Terrified, I dance still faster until I am out of the ballroom and into the forest of despair alone by myself, utterly fatigued and miserable. I play dead until I see still another delightful person, and begin the process all over again.

The same pattern occurs in spirituality. I build up to some sublime dance for a few weeks or months, and then find myself more and more exhausted and depleted. Despair. Then the gleam of some new illumination. The dance of the red shoes begins again.

2. What makes the red shoes so attractive? My mother is a person with great *joie de vivre*. She used to describe events in her past in glowing terms. My father has a very high-strung, excitable temperament. He used to play vivid, passionate music at top volume on the phonograph when we were children.

This marvelous mood, however, had little reference to our daily life, which followed the usual slow pace of school and play. Like most teenagers, I was confused and unformed, longing for ebullient experiences, but with energies not focused enough at the time to sustain intensity.

As soon as I began to find myself as a philosophy student and develop more intense relationships with friends at college, I threw myself into the rhythm of the red shoes, happy to be able finally to live! Now as a wife and mother and professor, the "red shoes" part of life is a welcome contrast to the tedium of household chores and teaching lows.

3. Who played or now plays the role of the soldier or the shoemaker tempting me to put on the red shoes? No human person. Everyone I know who loves me tries to stop me from putting on

the red shoes. Everyone is eager to calm me down. My friends and my family are sometimes alarmed at the fatigued state I get myself into. They also have to suffer from my annoyance at having to take off the red shoes to do slowly paced work.

I sometimes think it is the devil himself who offers me the red shoes. He offers me Eve's apple—promising me extraordinary highs of intellectual illumination if I put on the red shoes. He promises me the delights of the early Mary Magdalene if I will put on the red shoes of emotional frenzy. He promises me the ecstasy of the mystics if I will pursue the spiritual life at an even greater speed.

4. Who gets sacrificed to my need to dance? The old lady of the Andersen version, whom Karen neglects in order to go to the ball, represents family members whom I neglect in the rapid pursuit of my projects.

Concretely, this takes the form of shooing them out of the room or yelling at them when they interrupt me. I put the family in second place to concentrate on new, stimulating friendships. I choose to pray when I should be doing works of love.

Although happily married to a man who affirms me in my work and religious goals, when conflicts arise I find myself, like Moira Shearer in the movie, neglecting some deep need of my husband in favor of the pursuit of my own "dance."

5. What would I have to "cut off" to be free of the red shoes? Sometimes I imagine that I must give up my writing and just do household chores and plodding aspects of university work, even give up prayer meetings and retreats.

At such a thought, I go into a deep funk. During periods when my creative work has gone stale, when I have no special I-Thou relationship to pursue, and when my spiritual life is going along in a solid but uneventful manner, I become so restless that I am unbearable, to myself as well as to others.

No one who counsels me has ever suggested that I should renounce my creative work, or my friendships, or my prayer times. The ideal seems to be not to cut off my feet to be rid of the red shoes but, instead, to learn to dance more slowly and rhythmically.

6. Who is the angel who can bring me to the heaven of peace?

For me, Mary Magdalene is the patron saint who herself was brought out of the whirlwind of her own temperament and life choice to the stillness of adoration at the feet of the Lord.

When I take off the red shoes long enough to sit at the feet of Christ in prayer, the same peace comes to me. To do so, I must hold fast to move time in his presence at Mass and afterward. I must really take off the red shoes by putting all my projects and relationships into his hands and concentrating only on God himself, letting him speak to me, come right within me at communion. I rest at his feet, washing them with my tear-stained hair, and move into his wide heart, where I can be wife, mother, teacher, writer without any conflict.

When I leave the chapel, I put on the red shoes again, but I can dance in them much more slowly, falling into rhythm with God's dance of life.

Here are questions for your response:

1. What do the red shoes represent in your life—past, present, or future?

2. What makes the red shoes so attractive?

3. Who played or now plays the role of the tempting soldier or shoemaker who convinces you of the magic of the shoes?

4. Who is being sacrificed to your need to "dance" without cease?

5. Can you take off the red shoes? To be free of the red shoes, what would you have to cut off?

6. Is there someone who can play the role of the angel in your life, saving you from the consequences of your frenzies and bringing you to a heaven of peace?

Response to the Red Shoes

MARY NEILL

The line of the fairytale that struck my heart was, "In heaven no one questioned her about the red shoes." It highlights for me what is often the central need for each of us: how, on earth, shall I be "confirmed?" (Note how confirmation sets the stage for Karen's fall.)

How can I be confirmed for all the opposites in me, mortal in this dangerous world—opposites etched in this tale as rich lady/poor orphan; red shoes/black shoes; going to church/going to a ball; individual worship/congregational worship.

These opposites often bring on our deepest warfare and we are tempted inwardly and outwardly to cut one side out, i.e., to decide, "I'm going to have a ball and never go to church" or "I will always wear what others consider appropriate and never stand out from the crowd." We all endure the cycles these opposites play in us—endure them more or less consciously, more or less painfully. Jungian psychology describes this phenomenon as *enantiodromia,* the law of opposites, i.e., that everything leads to its opposite as the soul seeks wholeness, as it seeks equilibrium. There is a time for red shoes—a time to be free, to whirl about. I think we tend to get stuck in either black shoes or red shoes because we have denied (or been denied) the positive core of each.

It is hard for orphans to dance—so much poverty, sadness, insecurity, and loneliness. The adamantine hold the red shoes have for Karen comes from the vacuum created by their previous prolonged denial.

It is as if there is an inner law of retribution—of vengeance, which if we reflect upon we must seek to change into the law of love—as the Old Testament notions of an eye for an eye and a tooth for a tooth move toward forgiving he who has injured you, even seventy times seven times.

As you love your neighbor as yourself, so love your red shoes as part of yourself; your black shoes as part of yourself; don't choose between them, casting the rejected part to the devil; don't choose between body and soul. Christ didn't choose to be God and not man; nor man and not God. Endure and love the opposites—their wholeness, hidden from you, but united in God.

The saddest part of the story for me is the cutting off of her feet; notice that it doesn't take away the demonic energy of the symbol; rather it seems to cauterize it in her mind. I know that Christ said that "If thy eye offend thee, pluck it out," pointing thereby to a necessary season and time for cutting away, letting go, pruning extraneous baggage. But I think red shoes are not extraneous baggage. I see his admonition as warning us to cut out poisonous aspects of our vision that prevent us from seeing as God sees us, loving as God loves, wholly and mercifully, embracing the opposites he created, the sun by day, the moon by night: "In his image he made them; male and female he made them" (Gen. 1:27). He made us feet fit for black shoes and red shoes; he made us to dance and to slough along; to be free and to be bound; to live forever and to die.

The perfect fathering consciousness that God has, that we are called to have and to spread, on earth as it is in heaven, is one that embraces opposites: "In heaven no one questioned her about the red shoes."

It is our desire to control life and its opposites, to be lords of the dance that is death-dealing in that dread inner death which lends its horror to our body's decay (and not vice versa).

I feel that when we fail to give and receive deep confirmation for the opposites intrinsic to mortality, then we are in danger from being burned up by the extremes, of being given over to the demonic, shadow side that each instinct has when we have not brought this part, red or black, to Christ for his blessing and naming—it thrashes us about. Black shoes can be demonic, too.

Christ cast out demons by his loving consciousness—he had both the Virgin Mary and the Prostitute Mary to witness his death and resurrection, the dutiful daughter and the dancing daughter—the white and the red. He is the Lord of the dance, not we.

Now add any additional images of your own in your journal.

⚜ Goldilocks
The Trying, Tripartite Search

MARY NEILL

Very recent in its origins (nineteenth century), Goldilocks is an unusual fairytale, ending with neither recovery nor consolation. It is an ambiguous story, and a popular one—just recently I heard a sung version performed in a summer-camp program.

What are some of the implications of this simple story of a young girl lost in the forest, three times knocking on the three bears' house, three times trying to find the right food, three times trying to find the right chair, three times trying to find the proper bed? Three times three each of the three bears cries at the invasion of his/her privacy and territory. At the ninth cry, Goldilocks is awakened from sleep and runs away, neither found, helped, nor saved. A lost stranger once more.

The bears, though closely related to one another, do not relate to Goldilocks—she is an alien intruder. Her golden hair does not charm them; her distress does not move them. Whether she recovered some inner gift from this encounter is never made clear. Maybe what is clearer to the reader is a sense of the deep and long struggle each of us must endure to find our true identity—to find the soup, the chair, the bed—the living space, the home, aptly built for ourselves and no one else.

In her search, Goldilocks poses a danger to the order of the bears' world: "Who's been eating my porridge? Sitting in my

39

chair? Sleeping in my bed? Who's been destroying the order of my life—its food and furniture?"

The tree bears perhaps represent an archetype of human order. If the pyramid is a most stable and ancient architectural form, so the triangle is that relational form from which all life's stabilities evolve. A mother and a father produce a third, their child. There are three's everywhere. All stories have a beginning, a middle, and an end. Most all languages have a past, present, and future tense; a first, second, and third person. The Greeks saw the world governed by Zeus in heaven; Poseidon in the sea; Hades, underground. The dogma of the Trinity has impressed itself on Western Christian consciousness. Hegel's theory of history describes its movement as thesis, antithesis, synthesis. Freud named the stages of maturation as oral, anal, genital. One can go on and on finding three's everywhere, in the clover and out. Doubtless the number three must represent something in our psyche—a process that we all go through which involves some difficulty and danger to us and our world before its turbulence is resolved.

In the Bible, we see mankind begin in a garden which contains a man, a woman, and a snake. We see man fall into a desert of alienation whose gift is the promise of a Messiah who will lead man from the desert of alienation to the building of the heavenly city so hauntingly described in the Apocalypse; a city where God himself will wipe away the tears from our eyes, where "There will be no more death, no more grief, crying or pain" (Rev. 21:4). Home, where lostness and searching have come to an end. Garden, desert, heavenly city—three psychic spaces in our journey.

The journey after the fall is long and hard and what we bring forth is under the garden-curse of the sweat of our brow and the anguish of travail. We wander, closed from Paradise by a flaming sword. We try and try and try; and often what we confront or accomplish is too large—too hot, too hard, too tilted, as was the father bear's bed. It is too masculine, we are burned by it, as we are by the sun's rays if they beat too close on our skins. Or in our journey, we may be injured by aspects of feminine consciousness—too soft, too cool, too tilted at the foot, as was the mother bear's bed. The moon rays leave us cold. "The moon's a harsh mistress," the song warns.

And yet we must be subjected to these opposites within us and without us in our life's journey. Occasionally the child in us (the child who carries the promise of the kingdom) finds us the food that is fitting and a bed just right for resting—but never for very long. The kingdom is not yet come. The child's chair breaks under us, or we are awakened to the truth that we are sleeping in a borrowed bed, and even though it suits us, we must be out the door and gone.

We are lost in the woods, we seek order. With difficulty we find it. Then we are commanded by life, by God's providence, to let it go; to search for our own home. Like Goldilocks, we fit that admonition of St. Paul that we are pilgrims and have here below no abiding city.

The repetition of stages—the cycle of creation (Father), conflict (Son), and resolution (Holy Spirit) never seems to cease.

We long for an orderly life where everyone, everything has its proper identity, food, and furniture. But the story of Goldilocks suggests that this longing for security and survival, for permanent possession is an animal instinct, something belonging to bears and not Goldilocks. The trinitarian image molded by God calls man to transcend even the most central and laudable natural instincts; calls us to move toward a golden nature, a "super" nature if you like—one transformed and purified, as gold is refined in a crucible. We are Goldilocks, not the three bears.

So the dialectic of the inner journey is characterized by a search for order and a call to a higher order; a gaining and a letting go, like the systole, diastole of our heart beat; like the breathing in and out of our lungs. Holding the breath is easy—and dangerous. Our temptation is always to long to stay in the soft bed of the resolved search and not to move out again on the pilgrimage to the Truth beyond truth. We are like those voyagers Buddha warned against, who foolishly, after they have used a raft to cross a stream, put the raft on their backs and so slow down their progress on land.

We cling to our raft, our earthly identity, though we are told in Revelation (2:17) and we in part believe that our true name is written in heaven; the name no one knows but God—the identity of our deepest self hidden in God. Until our search is resolved on that day when in the heavenly city we are called by that name, we are called to sit loosely with our identity, as does Goldilocks.

Notice we never learn Goldilock's name—only a description. (In the original version, 1849, she was called Silverlocks.)

Silverlocks does not carry the weightedness of gold, as poets like Housman tells us in lines about his golden friends such as: "By brooks too broad for leaping / The lightfoot boys are laid; the rose-lipt girls are sleeping / In fields where roses fade." I knew from childhood that princesses and princes are all golden-haired heirs to the kingdom and that I was called to be a princess—to have a kingdom. "In my Father's house, there are many mansions," Christ assures our noble desires (John 14:2).

What has been disconcerting to me is the difficulty of the journey—the false starts, the mistaken identity, the being lost in the woods, the feeling of being an intruder, an outsider looking in, even on my own life. I had imagined somehow that one might be able to journey securely, as it were in a club car, safe from repetition and removal.

I even once thought of the Church as my Eden here on earth that protected me, as it did not those outside its canopy, from the perils of lostness and the search for my true self.

By becoming a nun at seventeen, I took on a secure order of name, of food and furniture. That security, by the providence of God, has been shaken and I who entered what was then a "high security, low risk" environment have been called out of that soft bed. The Lord has asked me again, three times three, to let go of my expectations of what it *means* to be a nun, a believer, a woman. He has sent me trying all manner of food and furniture; given me rest and then called me out the door again. He has locked me out of an abiding house here below; he has confounded me with the realization that I, as all Christians, have no choice but to be like him who describes himself: "The foxes have dens, the birds have nests, but the Son of Man has nowhere to lay his head" (Matt. 8:20). Not even a tomb kept his body at rest. Nor will it mine, if I follow him, not as I once thought as a cheerleader to his action, but a doer of his word.

Jesus, whom I thought a noun, taught me that he is a verb. "Not everyone who says to me, Lord, Lord ..." (Matt. 7:21). A harder journey than I first thought; I had imagined that I was exempt; that he had wandered homeless so I wouldn't have to. Now I know that if I have in myself the mind that was his, a mind free to love and say Yes, I must tread the wine press and I am, basically, not gladdened (though there are moments). I am amazed; simply amazed, that he thinks that much of me, and of every Christian. "You overestimate my strength, Lord," I plead. "You underestimate your power," he says—"and the beauty of your golden locks."

Bruno Bettelheim thinks that Goldilocks is not a satisfactory tale because it is without resolution.[2] Satisfying it may not be, but neither is the ambiguity and tripartite searching that accompanies our personal journey. In homes and out, sharecroppers of life, tenant farmers in the Lord's vineyards, living on borrowed bread and bed, we are called to beyond, because we are Goldilocks, locked out of abiding security in this life; called to golden immortality, here in promise and beyond, in depth.

I wrote the following poem at the end of a long retreat, when I was surrounded by many Marys, inside me and out, in people, in scriptures. I was haunted by the thought that I am always searching for a Mary beyond this Mary. Read the poem, and then write one of your own, touching on your feelings about your search for identity.

Dark Mary, what is there but to follow that melody
However softly strummed in our frail flesh, that tune
Refrained from Christ's death entombing song, sung
First of all by those guardian Marys of his
Dead flesh—Marys Nazarene and Magdalene;
Of Bethany, of Cleophas—lovers / Virgins / widows
Who early, late; dark, or light—each in each
Each for each both lose and weep, find and keep—
But may not cling long in garden's dawning light
To that near Christ, to that far, fair Mary
Who ever goes before them into northern Galilee.

Your Reflections on Goldilocks

Now write your response to Goldilocks, if you wish, including answers to some of these questions:

1. What homes have you had to leave?

2. When did you first realize that you had golden locks—were a princess-heir?

3. What are your feelings about being a pilgrim (a person on a journey with no guarantee of a permanent place on earth)?

4. What are the times and places you feel (have felt) most lost in the wood? What do you do when you feel this way?

5. List all the names you have ever been called. What has been the "gift" of each one? Have you ever wanted to change your name? What names would you add to your name now? Why?

6. Write a dialogue with the Lord telling him how you feel about the difficulty of the journey. Ask him what he felt.

Response to Goldilocks

RONDA CHERVIN

Mary's thoughts about Goldilocks followed me all week. I did the exercises mentally and it was very easy to trace the search for a permanent home in my life. The basic ideas about Goldilocks are intriguing, making the reader view things from totally new angles. I tend to box myself into overly orderly categories—the bears vs. Goldilocks. There is some wonderful writing in it about club cars, being an outsider in one's own life (plight of creative people?), and the beauty of golden locks.

Regarding the concept of home, there seems to me to be a tension between two different models in spirituality. The first emphasizes detachment because no finite home really fits, only the eternal. A medieval saint wrote, "Happy the man who has a homeland, still better the man for whom every land is a home, but blessed the man who has no home but eternity." The second type envisions the earthly homes as incarnational images of the eternal home—"on earth as it is in heaven"—the family itself as

Christian community, not as a launching pad for the spiritual journey alone to the great alone.

For example, the homemaker tries to fix up her house-beautiful into a perfect image. This may lead her to hate all that is imperfect—dirt (eyes are on your floors, ring around the collar), machines that break, and even her own children and husband may be conceived of as those who refuse to fall into her plans for the ideal.

For the woman working outside the home, the tension between seeing life as a pilgrimage or as a little kingdom takes some unexpected forms. For instance, if she discovers she does not fit into the great Mother chair dispensing food and warmth, she is propelled out of the home into the world. At first she may draw energy for this feat from the denigration of the hearth and the despising of the simple animal needs of family people as philistine.

But at work she also has a hard task. Her feminine homemaking instinct may sneak up on her as she tries without success to transform the office, the school, the world, from a competitive arena into a community. Some resolve this by drifting into jobs where "motherly" service is appreciated—such as quietly and sweetly doing the chores that make it possible for some man to go out and fight the dog-eat-dog battles!

As the career woman tries to come to grips with the tension between her desire for permanent homey structures and the transitoriness and dynamic shifts of the world outside, I see her adopting a variety of unsuccessful stances such as these:
—desperate attempts to reform the world, followed by bitterness at failure.
—seeking pockets of warmth in a cold world through overly intense office friendships.
—setting oneself up as a perpetual critic—damning the home while at work and the work environment while at home.
—moving from job to job seeking the perfect spot.
—trying out bigger and better roles in hopes of controlling things more: I, "Papa-Boss," will make you all act like human beings, or I, "Mama-Boss," will tell Papa unless you do everything I say.

Defeat finally leads to childish regression where one fantasizes about becoming a perpetual student by going back for still another degree, finding some lowly secure job with no impossible challenges, or hiding under the wings of some powerful person who will tell you what to do moment by moment. For some, escape is sought in alcohol, or drugs, or sex.

What I have written is realistic but surely not the final word. If woman by her very nature will tend to try to make life more homelike, perhaps she has to keep trying in spite of her knowledge that all earthly things are imperfect. The energies she might otherwise put into blaming others for the surrounding evils or in fantasies of utopia can be gradually deflected into the important task of doing her best day by day.

When tempted to give up in my vain attempts at homemaking in the narrower and broader sense, my best source of replenishment of energy is going into my "closet" to pray to God. There I experience the sheltering presence of the Father of the kingdom, am emboldened by the thought of the suffering Savior, and filled with new life by the Spirit.

Any additional reflections?

⚜ Dorothy and the Wizard of Oz

RONDA CHERVIN

As we open the famous classic of L. Frank Baum, written in 1900, we find Dorothy, a normal young girl, living in Kansas in the shadow of her hardworking but grim pioneer aunt and uncle with only her dog, Toto, for a companion in fun.

A cyclone comes. Dorothy and Toto run into the storm cellar, but not in time. The twister sends the whole house up in the air and lands them in the fairytale land of the Munchkins.

Dorothy discovers she is in a place menaced by witches, but the good witch gives her a magic kiss and tells her that if she ever wants to return to Kansas she must go on a long journey in search of the famous Wizard of Oz.

On her way with her little dog, Toto, she meets the scarecrow without a brain, the tin woodman without a heart, and the cowardly lion without a strong will, and on they all go down the yellow brick road in search of the mysterious land of Oz, from which they expect all things.

On the road the group have many adventures—too many to detail here. The only one I will deal with symbolically is the field of beautiful poppies that lulls Dorothy to a sleep from which she is saved by her friends.

Finally, Dorothy and her strange crew get to Oz. They are told they can only see the Wizard one by one alone. The guards are amazed at Dorothy's courage in wanting to see the fearsome Oz. The throne room contains a chair with an enormous head on it with no body. Dorothy begs to be allowed to go back to Kansas. The Wizard says she must first kill the wicked witch of the West.

With fear and trembling, Dorothy and her companions set off to find the wicked witch. The evil witch tries to destroy them. The scarecrow and the tin woodman battle to the death trying to save Dorothy. The captured Dorothy finally defeats the witch's clever stratagems, not through her own guile but through an impulsive act of throwing water at the witch, making her melt to nothingness. The tin woodman and the scarecrow are "resurrected." They return to get their reward and discover that Oz is not a great wizard but only a man pretending to be God. They realize that the intelligence, heart, and courage they seek is within themselves to develop. Finally, Dorothy returns to Kansas with the help of the good witch, Glinda. The picture on the last page of the book shows her happy to be home with Toto and in the arms of a loving Aunt Em.

As soon as I started to write this inner-exploration piece, I realized that I have a real love-hate relationship to the famous Dorothy. Every time my children turn on the Judy Garland movie on television, I leave the room—yet find myself humming "Somewhere over the rainbow" very often!

This may seem strange. How could anyone not simply love Dorothy as a sweet, courageous symbol? Can it be that I both cherish and despise the naive, vulnerable little girl within my own adult self?

As I proceed with my analysis, it will become more apparent why the image of Dorothy is so ambiguous to me—perhaps for you, too.

Let me begin with the repressive Aunt Em and Uncle Henry, whom I see as symbols of my own parents at times when they would finally lose patience with their giddy twin girls (myself and my sister) and insist on law and order.

Actually, my parents were tolerant of our childish play, and perhaps it was because they were rather permissive that we would become stunned if they ever forced us to obey. I remember finding it inconceivable that adults did not want to spend their time playing with us children instead of doing dull chores.

I see myself now as a parent being much more like Aunt Em

than my own mother was! Loving the peace and order conducive to study, I found the giddiness of my own twin daughters when they were small to be almost unbearable. Occasionally, I would relax and get into their fun, but mostly I would gaze on them with dismay because they were making it impossible for me to spend my time in philosophical thought or contemplative prayer!

My anger at their natural high spirits would reach an apex at times of direct conflict of interests, such as just before bedtime when their riotous play would postpone the beginning of my blessed quiet time, or when interesting guests would come to dinner and I would have to leave in order to discipline the children. Most painful of all was taking the children to Sunday Mass. Having to suppress their antics prevented me from deep recollection in prayer so their presence would come to seem like some sort of purgatory.

My own need to be a carefree girl having fun even as an adult seems to erupt in ways I am never sure I approve of.

Perhaps because the child in me is suppressed by having too much work to do as wife, mother, professor, and writer, when some funny situation arises or even a casual joke, I will go off into gales of laughter.

If I meet anyone who is able to make me laugh, I will sometimes neglect duties to make the most of this unexpected possibility of childlike freedom, and then feel guilty about tasks undone.

I have a special affection for any student who can make the others laugh, and if I have a class with many humorous students, I will sometimes quite forget scholastic aims and just join in the fun, to the chagrin of the more serious students who don't happen to like the style of the extroverts.

Of late, I have begun to laugh at myself more. Having accomplished many of my career goals and realized their relativity, I am more willing to take time to relax, play games with my teenage twins or with my son, go out with my husband, and enjoy light conversation with friends instead of insisting on "deep" communication.

Are there any Aunt Em's and Uncle Henry's in my life right now? Yes, I realize, somewhat to my surprise. When joking with one person, I see in the background the faces of others not part of the joy who seem to me to be gazing at me censoriously and sometimes a bit enviously. Their seeming disapproval of my raucous laughter makes me imagine that I am guilty of some crime.

Their faces remind me of some elementary schoolteachers who naturally had to control us if any schoolwork was to be done. In school you get gold stars for being quiet, orderly, and getting your work done, never for being joyful and fun-loving.

There is a certain association in my mind of orderliness, neatness of dress, controlled low voice, with primness and repressiveness, so that when I even see someone having any of these characteristics, I tend to imagine they will disapprove of my free, hoydenish ways. Often I find that these very people wish they could be more spontaneous and vivacious.

Recently I was at a special church celebration. Most of the participants were rather stiff and formal. I found myself becoming almost claustrophobic in their presence. I wanted to run around the church and sing and dance in the spirit of the actual joyful words of the liturgy—to do something wild to break away from the corpselike rigidity of the people. The very next day, I attended a charismatic Mass in the same chapel. I was delighted by the spontaneity and freedom of the people. Here we could wear bright-colored clothes, comfortable shoes, sway and raise our hands in prayer, and sing loudly and passionately with no one to frown at us and keep us in line.

Another image from the Wizard, the magic kiss of the good witch, reminds me of those in the church I view as being hollow, brainless scarecrows, rusty tinmen who have no hearts and cannot love, and cowardly lions.

With the fiery zeal of the convert, I would rouse the mediocre and save the world, as Joan of Arc saved France. Needless to say, my militant stance produces resistance even in the seemingly lifeless. Is it that they rightly sense the fanaticism threatening to poison the zeal, or do they fear that the truths of the church may turn out to be no more worthy of adoration than Oz? If either of these two explanations is correct, I have no right to scorn them. Either I must change and become less militant, or I must witness to the truth in ways doubters might find more convincing.

To me, the most intriguing adventure of Dorothy occurs in the deadly field of poppies.

> They walked along listening to the singing of the brightly colored birds and looking at the lovely flowers which now became so thick that the ground was carpeted with them. There were big yellow and white and blue and purple blossoms, besides great clusters of scarlet poppies, which were so brilliant in color they almost dazzled Dorothy's eyes. . . . Now it is well known that when there are many of these flowers together, their odor is so powerful that anyone who breathes it falls asleep. And if the sleeper is not carried away from the scent of the flowers, he sleeps on and on forever.

Dorothy succumbs to the spell cast by the beauty of the poppies, and the tin woodman and the scarecrow make a chair of their arms and carry her away, still asleep. They lay her on the ground and wait for a fresh breeze to waken her.

For me, the beautiful but deadly poppies represent the lure of the sensual deflecting me from the path of working for "the cause," in my case the "good news" of my faith. This sensuality can take the form of longing to sleep and sleep, to drown in the fantasies of romantic novels, to daydream about a totally different and irresponsible life-style, and even to misuse the gift of contemplation as an escape from life instead of the deepened surrender to God *and* the work he has given me in the world.

When I succumb to these temptations, my spiritual advisers and brothers and sisters in the faith carry me away, arouse me by teaching me the truth and eventually God sends a fresh breeze in the form of some new challenge.

Who is the wicked witch that I must conquer in order to continue my journey?

I think that the wicked witch is probably not some external figure, but rather my own self-hatred. In opening this section I wrote that I had a love-hate relationship to Dorothy. Probably there is a witch (bitch?) in me who hates the idealistic Dorothy and would prefer just to destroy everyone, including myself, in wrathful frustration.

My faith suggests to me that I accept even martyrdom in the

cause of love rather than become a witch-bitch. In fact, the witch-bitch can be defeated by so ordinary and unexpected re-birth in the waters of baptism, the cleansing action of the sacra-ment of reconciliation, the transformed body of the loving Lord in Holy Communion.

Like the scarecrow and the tin woodman, I can be given a new mind, reformed from worldly shrewdness to the truths of God, and a new heart, formed in the image of the sacred hearts of Jesus and Mary, and the true, not fanatical but holy, courage of Joan of Arc.

The Wizard?

In my life, the phony Wizard is not the God of religion, but rather the false idols I would worship instead—human beings I imagine have all the strength to bring me "home" but instead are as weak and fallible as I am. I must develop my gifts instead of trying to lean on them. I must love the "phonies" for their real selves as brothers and sisters.

The good witch Glinda represents to me sisters in the Lord who do not try to be idols but instead help me to love myself—how many the Lord has sent me!

Home is heaven—the perfect kingdom of love the Father has prepared for those who love him.

Response

1. When you, the reader, were a child, were your girlish de-lights appreciated by your parents or did you feel repressed?

2. Who plays the role of Aunt Em or Uncle Henry in your life now? When do you get a chance to be a carefree little girl?

3. In your woman's tale, what is the magic kiss that gives you strength in times of fear?

4. What people in your life seem to you to be like scarecrows in need of stuffing, tin woodmen who need oil, and cowardly lions?

5. When propelled by a strong vision for the future, do you ever become fanatical? Do you think the causes you fight for are worth all the zeal you expend on them?

6. In your life, what acts as a beautiful but sleep-producing drug tempting you away from your mission? Who are the com-panions who rescue you from such deadly drugs? Describe fresh

breezes that have given you a new impetus during past times of wanting to give up.

7. In your life, who do you think of as the wicked witch? What unexpected things save you from her?

8. When have you been given a new mind, heart, or courageous will?

9. Who have been phony Oz figures in your life, or people who turned out to be disappointing because you overestimated them?

10. What women have been Glinda to you?

11. What is home?

Response to the Wizard of Oz

MARY NEILL

I was a sober child, nicknamed "grandmother" at five, so I start when questioned about the carefree little girl in me. My parents were not "repressive" of fun—their humor has been a rich inheritance for me. I simply was that kind of child early on whose nature was to parent my parents, to try to take care of them and the world. I repressed my own little inner child; I did not need any help.

It was after entering the convent that my inner child was freed to play, to counteract my grimness of purpose. All my closest friends seem to have a wild child in them that adds joy to my life and their own. One of the advantages of convent life is that you do not have to be very wild at all to get an Aunt Em reaction. One of the most satisfactorily disruptive acts I have ever seen was that of a nun friend (carefully trained as we all were never, never to even so much as check the candy on the second layer of a box of sweets, much less take a piece from that forbidden place) who politely selected a piece of candy at formal recreation, took a bite, and threw it over her shoulder, à la Henry VIII, saying, "Ugh, marzipan." It was sufficiently outrageous, innocent, and riotous to be well-received. A friend like that is a treasure for life, as well as dangerous.

Our wild child has a gift to give not only ourselves, but others. When Christ says, "Unless you become as a child, you shall not enter the kingdom," I cannot imagine his excluding those children whose pushing through to him was wild enough to annoy the disciples.

What has been the magic kiss of strength for me? I think it was my parents' faith in God, in the ultimate goodness of mankind, and in me. Whatever my trials, I was good, was special, would succeed and survive. This faith in myself, in my life, in the world, in God, is an incredible legacy for which I am increasingly grateful through the years. As a child, to feel my mother's body praying; as an adult to see my father's devotion at Mass—this is indeed a magic kiss. If in the distress of life I am undermined, it is because I choose, like the prodigal son, to squander my inheritance and feed on the husks of pain and disbelief in myself, in the world, in God.

Who are the scarecrows, the tin woodmen, and the cowardly lions in my life? I tend to be so critical that it feels dangerous to answer this question other than by referring to my own unfinished parts—my lack of guts, of heart, of flexibility. But I have come to know that it is an act of moral courage to speak out against evils others don't see, or that they take for granted.

I feel that the greatest dangers in the church and religious life center around cultivating fear, honoring cowardice, and disowning the "reasons of the heart." I see men and women afraid to embrace the dying of old forms, or the loss of their own security or power, and so disbelieving in resurrection. I see many refusing to trust their heart, using logic and "principles" as reasons for refusing to relate to someone or to some group alien in thought and life-style; I see profound cowardice in refusing to build bridges. In fact, I see a lot of bridge-bombing.

I do not want to name churchmen and churchwomen as unique in this cowardice and "heart" failure. The film, *Autumn Sonata,* brought home to me how we religious are merely taking on the pessimistic, nonrelational coloration of our culture, we who are vowed to be countercultural. This film contains the most violent scene I have ever witnessed. The good, plain daughter, Eva, confronts her glamourous, shallow mother, Charlotte, with evidence of the evil scars of hatred and rejection her mother's rearing has brought on her. The mother sees the hatred, sobs and asks forgiveness. The daughter sits icy and unmoved, enclosed in her own pain; she will not forgive her mother's moral flimsy. She will not see the mother's suffering as her own. She will not build a bridge.

Eva will not own herself a sinner, for she is the good girl, married to a parson, keeper of her spastic sister, organ player at church. The daughter gives herself the right to hate—not to forgive—she has bought the right through her moral goodness and her pain. She can be good to the obedient weak who depend on her; she cannot be good to the independent.

I see many priests, religious women, and other "good" Christians acting out of the same horrifying vision: "I lead a good life. I don't have to forgive, to hear the 'reasons of the heart.' My principles are too strong for that. It is all right for a Christian to hate his enemy—and to show this hate in icy disdain."

To write this saddens me. I consider this lack of forgiveness, this failure to live the final promise of the Our Father, as the major obstacle to renewal in the church. I am not fanatical by nature, or even zealous, but I could become fanatical about this carrion corruption of nonforgiveness that eats at the heart of Christian communities—and world peace. But if I do not forgive, try to bridge to those who are unforgiving by nature or choice, to try to relate to their small island (for surely such a vision shrinks them small) am I not a double hypocrite—unforgiving of the forgiving? Such is the double bind of the gospel message.

Who tempts me from my mission? Who/what rejuvenates me? I let myself be drugged by too much of everything—food, books, people, work, talk, excessive activity, then excessive need to rest. My motto: "Anything worth doing is worth overdoing" ultimately does not console. I think that under all these symptoms of despair (for they are a kind of despair) I fear greatness. I do not want success. I can't explain why I think this is the answer, but when Ernest Becker described the "Jonah syndrome" in his *Denial of Death*, it struck home. Like Jonah, when I hear the call to serve God specially and bear the trials of honoring his word in me whatever the difficulties involved, I get on a ship and head the other way. Like Jonah, I am thrown from my ship. I hide in the belly of the whale and when finally I get the word out, I sulk under a tree because the word is successful.

Companions who confirm my vocation by their response, the many graces of loving affirmation that rain upon me when I preach the good news, these help turn my pouting "no" into a scared "yes," and put me back on the yellow brick road.

Who is my wicked witch? My hypercritical harassing inner tape that says, "You're not good enough"; "Nothing's good enough." This hard voice is dissolved many ways—the waters of tears (my own and my friends', or others whom my hardness hurts); the waters of the truth that it just isn't so that I or anyone has to be perfect.

My phony Wizard? Churchmen and churchwomen, or cultural gurus, whom I have endowed with magical powers of affirmation only to find that they have clay feet.

My good witch? The voice, inner or outer, that says, "Look down. Your salvation, your way back home, is at your feet!"

My home? I have to be honest and say that I do not know where it is—homelessness seems to be my lot. We lived in thirteen states before I was eight years old. The number of houses I have lived in is uncountable. I've never had a Kansas to go back to after the whirlwind. I think somehow that this is all right, because just as Dorothy has the key to home on her very feet—all she has to do is click her heels—I have a sense that home is always where I stand. Here I am. I need only own it as such—make myself at home there; to say, with Jacob, "*This* is the gate of heaven." "(Home) God is here, and I never knew it" (Gen. 28:17).

Any concluding images?

⚜ Cinderella

MARY NEILL

As you probably know already, there are many versions of the Cinderella story. Mary and Ronda each wrote about different renditions, so unalike that there will be a different set of questions for each.

Here is Mary's spinoff:

When Ronda and I divided up the fairytales prior to writing this workbook, I had no trouble "giving" her Cinderella for major treatment; it's too obvious, too popular, too saccharine. But I found that my hand and eye thought differently from my head, and "by mistake" I did this one, instead of the one assigned.

So my response to Cinderella is not response, but full-blown reflection. Cinderella wanted me, even if I didn't want her. Willful girl, that one.

I have come to trust such mistakes; to listen to them—to honor that my hand and heart know better than my head what needs to be done. "Pity that the head is slow to learn, what the swift heart beholds at every turn" is my rewording of St. Vincent Millay's sonnet line. Have you ever made mistakes such as this, which consume extra time and throw you off of plan? Do you trust this? How do you deal with it?

Cinderella is the most popular and ubiquitous of all fairytales—found all over Europe, Africa, and Asia. One scholar produced a study of 345 versions. A central theme, however, is common to all the versions: a young woman once held in high esteem falls from favor into degradation and then is given an exalted role in the end. She is recognized despite her tatters because of a slipper which fits only her foot. The Grimms' version I will comment on contains these additional details: the gift she asks of her father (a hazel branch she plants on her mother's grave); the birds who help her; the tree beside her mother's grave which provides her with the clothes for the ball; Cinderella's triple flight from it; the lost shoe; the shoe test; the sisters' mutilation of their feet to win acceptance; the warning of the birds; the vengeance on the wicked stepsisters by the birds who pluck out their eyes.

The version used by Disney, based on that of Perrault, seems to me rather too cleansed from violence; Cinderella far too passive to the abuse showered on her. The Grimms' Cinderella has more spunk and I like her better since feistiness in the face of abuse seems to me an important moral virtue.

The Cinderella tale strikes this central chord in me: the necessity of the endurance of loss of respect, of aloneness, of alienation and hard work in our soul's journey—the suffering each of us encounters because we are not confirmed and seen in our true worth by those who should—those we live with.

The hearth that should give us warmth and sustenance is the scene of our tattered clothes and ashes. We are left without an outer advocate. We feed as the scriptures say, on dust and ashes; like those Babylonian exiles, we cannot sing, but sit and weep in nostalgia for all the nurturing mother-love that once sustained us, but is no more. Like Cinderella, we weep on our mother's grave, without protection.

If we are lucky, we weep. For it seems to me that the tears feed the reality of the longing and so move us to search for that which is lost. All experience this loss; but not all can weep and they are the worse for it. In memory of her mother's love, Cinderella plants a tree (a tree of life) to grow from death. This tree later supplies her with the clothes for the ball, the dance, the marriage feast. Losing and weeping are prelude to finding and keeping. Before Easter, when the tree of death becomes a tree of life, comes the forty days of fasting, sackcloth, and ashes, the weeping for the sins which make the kingdom lost to us.

The Cinderella story reminds us that we are always under attack—the powers of loss, decay, selfishness eat at the goodness we have. To live means daily confrontation with loss and lack of love.

To be a heroine is to fight to regain what is lost, to confirm oneself in love, so that we must search, leave our hearth in order to find our love—to risk being found by him not only at the ball, a shining dancer, but in the ashes, a drone who wears tatters and is despised by some who know her well. If he is a true prince, he goes not by outer appearances but by what we stand on—our foot which fits the lost slipper. Such a prince, inner or outer, is not found without courageous searching and many tasks.

And what are the tasks that Cinderella performs which help in her transformation from rags to gold? (We may be degraded by accident, but in the spiritual kingdom we are not elevated by accident. Once graced with a wedding invitation, we must weave a wedding garment, or be thrown out in the darkness, as Jesus warns.)

Her first task was to remember what had once been. Faith, as Newman noted, is not to deny in the dark what one has seen in the light. She remembers and ritualizes her mother's nurturing love; thereby internalizing it, so that she could learn to do for herself what once her mother had done. Her fleshly mother gone, she had to live gladly, internally through her *god* mother. And Cinderella honored this memory not only by weeping, but by planting. Remembering is central to faith, as we hear the command at Eucharist: "Do this in remembrance of me." We are a people who remember Jesus and so become planters of life where death has been sown.

Secondly, she does all the annoying tasks set to her—helping the ungrateful sisters get ready for the ball, sorting out the lentils her stepmother twice throws in the ashes. She is patient, as the psalmist promises: "In patience, you shall possess your souls."

Thirdly, she not only is unafraid to cry, to live with aloneness—she is not afraid to ask for help. She asks her father for a gift; her godmother tree for clothes; the birds to help her sort the grain from the ashes. Though she is alone and harassed, she knows that she cannot make it alone; she must do all she can and also call for help, from nature itself.

Often, when I am sorrowing, I will not ask for comfort. So I am moved by the account of Christ's agony in the garden when he was not ashamed three times to ask for help. When his disciples fail him, he prays and an angel comes to comfort him. Have you

not sometime experienced comfort from nature, from inner consolation (the work of angels) when no friend outside stood by?
Faith is also believing that we have a right to receive help and
that if we ask extravagantly, even impudently, it will come.

Fourthly, she risks being happy again. She doesn't cling to her
sadness, to her identification with ashes and humiliation. She
works hard to get to the ball; she goes three times and dances until
dawn (only Perrault presses her to midnight return). She lets herself laugh and dance and be beautiful and vulnerable, even care-
less in the loss of her shoe.

We often cling to unhappiness as to an old identity it gives us.
The danger of suffering is that we may take it as our inheritance
and not as a season. Cinderella, though patient, is not passive. She
believes that she can find what was lost; she believes that she was
made to dance and to love—to be a finder and a keeper, and not,
in the end, a loser and a weeper.

Fifthly, she lets herself be found by love, as she is—part dancer,
part drone; part honored, part despised. Unlike her sisters, she
mutilates no part of herself to fit someone else's shoe. In the
Grimms' version, the sisters are blinded by the bird to live in
darkness. They obeyed only their fleshly mother—accepted only
the identity she gave them. Hence they are thrown into perpetual
darkness. They created a hell for Cinderella. They are put in their
own hell.

Perrault's version does not punish the wicked sisters—too grue-
some a detail for our violent age, which has rejected the law of
retribution, "an eye for an eye, a tooth for a tooth." But psycho-
logically understood, when we are evil, our psyche does make us
pay. We do not achieve inner harmony. We are blinded to reality.
We live in darkness. Our eyes for seeing the transcendent world
are ultimately plucked out. Cinderella could see and hope in her
darkness and she came to her kingdom. The wicked sisters would
not see inner values. They mutilated themselves through obedience to greedy worldly standards and so they are cast out into
darkness.

I trust the "hard saying" of the Grimms' version, as Jesus asked
his disciples to trust his hard sayings. Should children be protected from such hard versions, such hard sayings? Emphatically

not. They experience many hard things, loss, separation, rejection, rivalry, wounding. Cinderella assures them that a way can be found out of the hard things—a hard way, but one where what they do, or don't do, makes all the difference.

One of the loveliest parts of the story to me is that the happy ending finds her. She searches for the prince and flees; he searches and finds her. I have learned to trust such a pattern of activity and passivity, of doing and of waiting, of withdrawal and return. So, with God, it seems that we pray and seek and knock and do, and then we know we are searched for; we are awakened by love.

When the Prince, who has seen Cinderella first in golden robes, puts the glass slipper on her foot amid the ashes, then has their union solid foundation in the marriage of opposites; rags and silks have honored one another; poor and rich, female and male, "for better or for worse, in sickness and in health."

Of all the things that the Cinderella story urges me to do in my spiritual struggle, to remember, to work patiently, not to cling to sadness, not to mutilate my identity, to let myself be found by love, I find the last one the hardest. For it means letting go of how and when and with what face love shall meet me. I find that once I have my active energies up, I don't want to pull back, be passive, and wait. Maybe I am not sure I will be found—or that anyone is searching. Darkness is seductive.

Your Response

1. What times in your life have been sorting of lentils and grains? Where did you find help for this tedious work?

2. What things cause you to weep? What relationships have been purified for you through weeping?

3. I have too often been a stepsister to myself, all too eager to follow an identity thrust on me from without. What shoes have you worn that did not fit? What mutilations have you endured for man, rather than God?

4. What memories of nurturing love and confirmation from your childhood have been sustenance in the storm for you? Who have been your godmothers of confirmation for your deepest self?

5. When have you hid your tattered side from those you love? When have you run from being found by love?

⚜ Cinderella

RONDA CHERVIN

Why do some fairytales please generation after generation of readers? Working on *The Woman's Tale* has explained it for me. Some heroines are archetypes of every woman's experiences.

As we follow along the so familiar story of Cinderella we will once again bring up to consciousness that which lies behind our delight in this rags-to-riches story. This meditation on Cinderella lends itself to frequent writing in your journal.

"There once was a man who had a beautiful wife and one lovely daughter, Ella."

As a child when did you feel like a special, uniquely loved daughter?

Being a twin, I was rarely able to be alone in the center. It was always a "we" experience. "The girls." But we were unidentical twins and everyone could tell us apart. As with so many twins, we were very different in personality.

I remember best the experience of walking alone with my mother to the library. It became a sort of ritual. It was a ten-block trek carrying our maximum load of ten books each. I remember enjoying the sense of perfect rapport without the distraction of my sister's presence. On the way to the library we would talk about the books we had read—usually I read all my mother's books too. On the way back we would chat about the writers whose works we had selected and then stop en route for a treat of tea and buttered English muffins at the local luncheonette. I felt very grown-up and content.

It was this experience of being more central in a one-to-one relationship than in a triad of mother and twins that seems to have set up a pattern of always wishing for twosomes and disliking group situations where you have to struggle for attention.

I also had the same feeling of affirmation in good times with my twin. Like all sisters we fought a lot, but we also had hours and hours of carefree playing together. These sessions could only be pursued alone. As soon as mother came home the heavy hand of duty would intrude: "set the table, clean up your room," and so on.

To continue with the tale—Cinderella's mother dies and her father remarries. Her stepmother already has two daughters of her own. They make Ella do all the work. While they wear fine clothing, she is reduced to ragged garments full of dirt from cleaning out the ashes in the fireplace. Cruelly they nickname her Cinder-ella.

When have you let yourself be made into a slavish Cinderella? Go through different phases of your life such as childhood, marriage, work situations, to examine your feelings. Do you still sometimes let other people give you a "name" of their choosing?

The first instance of feeling like Cinderella that comes to my mind, is the time of my parents' divorce. My father remarried a beautiful woman with a poised, pretty daughter. This young girl was several years older than we at a time when we were feeling most gauche and insecure as do all preteens. Even though in this case the new wife and daughter tried their best to be very loving, we felt most uncomfortable and second-rate.

The birth of my own twin girls ushered in a similar period of distress. Before their coming I had been like a princess to my husband. Then, as the care of the babies became more and more demanding, I watched them become the little princesses and felt myself to be like a slave to these powerful rivals. They were the prized possessions to be dressed up and shown off and I was a background figure doing diapers and cleaning house. It seemed to me at times that I was becoming more tired and uglier in direct proportion to their flourishing beauty.

There is a recurrence at times of such feelings even now when the twins are fooling around and I am doing housework. I will sometimes fly out at them demanding that *they* be Cinderella so I can get a chance to be a lady of leisure.

When do you find yourself making others play the role of Cinderella?

The beautiful fairy godmother is central to the story. What women have played the role of helpful fairy godmother in your life?

Who have been my fairy godmothers? I first picture one grammar school teacher who made me her pet. I was the shortest and the youngest in the class. Even though I was rather mischievous and sometimes compared unfavorably to my quieter twin, this teacher loved me and made me feel special.

Women friends of my mother would sometimes become close to me also, and their admiration for my potentialities would help compensate for feelings of being a social failure at school because I was not part of the popular crowd.

The most important woman in my life besides my own mother was my godmother at the time of my conversion to the Catholic church at twenty-one. Leni Schwarz, the wife of one of my philosophy professors, herself also a convert from an agnostic Jewish background, had one child—a son. She took me in and poured motherly care on my newly reborn soul. For a long time just to be in her presence was to feel like a princess.

My attitudes toward womanhood underwent drastic changes during this period. To a person with my free-thinking background, Catholic moral teachings about premarital sex, contraception, and even abortion had seemed weird. Like most intellectual converts, I had to work my way to realization of the truth of the church's teachings by painful and finally enlightened step-by-step reasoning.[3] This cerebral process was strengthened by the women in the circle of friends surrounding the Catholic philosophers at Fordham University. These women were all highly intellectual, cultured, and many of them professionals.

All, even if not themselves mothers, had to me a very surprising reverence for the natural endowments of women. The birth of a baby within the group was a cause not only for the expected pleasure in the infant, but for spiritual awe that a new creature had come into the world. Even in the case of the late pregnancies of already-burdened mothers, there was never a feeling that the child's birth was a calamity. Empathy and helpfulness were always combined with a sense of the mystery of God's providence.

That femininity was a gift of God stayed with me all through the trials of my own motherhood. Often at the end of my strength from the strain of duties so different from those I was trained for in philosophy, I would visit people in my original circle of friends and their affirmation of creation and love would buoy me up. I would realize again that there need be no false alternative between the path of maternity and development of individual talents. God wanted me to give myself totally to husband and children and also totally to teaching, lecturing, and writing. The goodness of the sheer being of my children was not altered by my natural defects as a busy career-mother.

To turn to another question: What ordinary realities in your life, i.e., the pumpkins and the mice, sometimes become coaches and coachmen to carry you to the ball? Write your answer in your journal.

For my part, sometimes while doing housework I will gradually let go my Cinderella complaints and then experience the quiet satisfactions of domesticity. The furniture begins to glow with memories of family happiness. Each item seems special as being part of the life-tale of each child or of my husband. Gratitude comes over me for our relatively cross-free existence—no child has suffered any tragic illness; there is no alcoholic husband. I sometimes begin to dance and sing around the house. My prison has become a ballroom.

If you had a fairy godmother who could give you any garment you wished as a ball gown what would you choose? Give a detailed description of your dream dress explaining what image of self you long for in fantasy.

I have two fantasy dresses. One is a red and black gypsy dress, slightly tattered. I would wear my hair in shining curls down to my waist. In another vision I would be wearing a white waltz-length ballet costume and I would execute the graceful steps of Viennese dances with a charming partner. The music would speed up gradually until it became a gypsy dance.

Since my normal life-style is rather sedate and intellectual—that of professor, writer, mother, I suppose that such an image represents the hidden side of me longing for wild sensuality or pure graceful feminine beauty.

Before she leaves for the ball, the fairy godmother warns Cinderella that she must be home by midnight or all her finery will turn back to rags and her coach back into a pumpkin.

Cinderella goes to the ball. The prince sees her and falls in love at once. They dance together over and over again while the bad stepsisters watch enviously.

Who have been the princes in your life? Can you find any common characteristics among these princes? Are their faults inevitable results of their virtues?

Pondering this question at length may result in some surprises.

At the peak of your experience of dancing with the prince, have you enjoyed the knowledge of the envy of other women?

"Suddenly the clock begins to strike midnight." In your life what were given as rules to be obeyed with dire consequences if broken? When you broke the rules did you find yourself becoming ragged and humiliated?

Even though I was not religious as a teenager I did sense that there was some sort of law against going too far sexually. Breaking this taboo at first seemed very liberating, but ultimately being rejected by lovers who had seemed so princely caused extremely destructive experiences of anguish. I found it very difficult to understand that the intoxication of love was simply not sufficient for life commitments, which neither I nor my boyfriends were willing to make. It was not until I became a Catholic that I could begin to make sense out of this pattern, to realize that grabbing forbidden fruit leads not to permanent residence but to exile from Eden.

So, Cinderella flees from the ballroom, losing one glass slipper. She returns home. Outwardly she is still Cinderella in rags, but of course her inner life is full of images of glory.

Can you remember periods in your life of outward tedium but inward daydreaming? Looking backward, what type of daydreaming seems healthy to you and what type an escape? When have you preferred daydreaming to life?

I smile now at memories of myself fantasizing about my husband-to-be, or about what each baby would be like. These fantasies were connected with future states really possible. On the other hand, I feel ashamed of fantasies which turned out to have no basis in reality. It makes me feel foolish to think of them, and guilty when they have focused around escape from the hard but good life of commitment God has called me to.

While Cinderella is dreaming of the prince she is busy at her normal household tasks. I picture her doing them this time without resentment because she knows that she has transcended the image of being "only a slave."

Under what conditions can you imagine yourself doing the jobs you find most slavelike but in a calm spirit because you know you have a "name" better than that of "slave?"

There was a very difficult time in my life when I was able nonetheless to do a lot of pesky work without anger. At that period my husband was deathly ill with severe asthma. My prince an invalid! Our twins were two and a half—a most difficult age. Brought to a state of real depression by the frustration of my daily existence, which seemed to be totally joyless, I was led to read St. John of the Cross. This writer emphasizes total detachment from pleasure as the only way to achieve peace. Deeply struck by the logic of his thought and touched by the beauty of his poetic writings, I decided to give up all hope of happiness and live only to do God's will.

For a month or so I was able to tend the children, stay up all night helping my husband over his attacks, without the usual feelings of self-pity.

Even though I was not able to sustain this state of spirituality, the memories of that time function as a peak experience of the possibility of deep peace coming from purity of heart. In terms of the Cinderella image, because God was calling me not miserable housewife but instead his bride, I could do everything menial with a renewed spirit.

The story of Martha in the Gospels also plays a large role in my self-image. Jesus chides Martha for being so activist that she has no peace. But Martha became a saint. Between the time when she was "busy and troubled about many things, but not attentive to the most important one" she must have learned to be a loving servant of God and man. She must have been just as generous in her hospitality but so anchored in contemplation of God that she did not drive herself and others into the ground.

Of course we all know the happy ending of Cinderella. Mary Neill asked about squeezing oneself into roles that don't fit. My example would be my dream of being a perfect Catholic mother with thirteen children. By the time the twins reached two years old I realized that I would be at best a shrewish though affectionate mother. I could never succeed in doing it beautifully—no glass shoes, only tattered bedroom slippers. I remember one day coming up with the astonishing thought "There are some things so important to do that even to do them badly is worthwhile." With this insight came the desire to have as many children as possible because they were so beautiful even if I could never handle the role well.

What would represent to you living happily ever after? Is forgiveness of the evil stepmothers and stepsisters in your life a necessary condition for inner happiness?

For me living happily ever after will come gradually the more I make Christ my prince and accept the fact that other "princes" are not to be worshiped but instead to be loved as fallible brothers.

Concluding Images—At this point do you have any final statement or symbol to put in your notebook? Rethink the questions posed throughout this section and write down your feelings about them.

⚜ Rapunzel

MARY NEILL

This fairy tale of the young girl locked in a tower by the wicked witch is not only one of my favorites, but that of many of the sisters with whom I live. I like pulling apart its threads and seeing what it reveals to us of ourselves.

The story goes like this: A man and a wife who had long waited for a child finally are blessed with that prospect. The wife during her pregnancy has an insatiable craving for the rampion that grows next door in the garden of a powerful witch. (Rampion is a member of the turnip family. It has a lovely flower and thick, edible roots.)

The husband steals the rampion, but eating it only increases his wife's craving. On his third venture, he is accosted by the witch who demands the forthcoming child in exchange for the rampion. Frightened, he consents. He later gives the child to the witch, who names her Rapunzel (rampion).

Rapunzel is the most beautiful child under the sun. When she is twelve years old, the witch shuts her up in a tower that stands in a wood. It has neither staircase nor doors, but only a little window, quite high up in the wall. When the witch wants to enter the tower, she stands at the foot of it and cries: "Rapunzel, Rapunzel, let down your hair!" (How I loved this line, as a child!)

A young prince hears Rapunzel, imprisoned in her tower, singing in her loneliness. Overhearing how the witch-stepmother gains access, he calls out the proper words and himself climbs her golden hair.

Rapunzel is first terrified and then charmed by the prince for she has never before set eyes on a man. They plan together for her to plait a silken ladder of her hair, little by little, until she can climb down it and escape with him.

The prince comes to her every evening. The witch comes in the daylight. One day Rapunzel naively says to the witch, "Tell me, Mother Gothel, how can it be that you are so much heavier than the young prince who will be here before long?" The witch, in a rage to realize that she cannot separate the child from the world, cuts off Rapunzel's golden hair and takes her away into a wilderness, to live in grief and misery.

When the prince comes, the witch lets down the plaits for the prince to climb and mocks him with wicked eyes. "You have come to fetch your ladylove, but the pretty bird is no longer in her nest. And she can sing no more, for the cat has seized her and it will scratch your own eyes out too."

The prince jumps from the window in grief and his eyes are scratched out by the thorns among which he falls. He wanders blind for many years until he reaches the wilderness where Rapunzel has been living in great poverty.

He hears a voice which sounds familiar to him and goes toward it. Rapunzel knows him at once and falls weeping upon his neck. Two of her tears fall upon his eyes and they immediately grow quite clear and he can see. The prince takes Rapunzel to his kingdom, where they live happily ever after.

Though the story is short, a mere three pages, compressed in it are the themes that haunt each of us: longing for new life, insatiable hunger, betrayal by fear, imprisonment, loneliness, blindness, searching, tears, reconciliation.

Rapunzel's conception and betrayal by her parents' weaknesses reminds me how each of us suffers from the result of original sin. Through human weakness and frailty, a part of us is orphaned by our parents. They bring to life in us what they know how to, but the other part or parts are ignored, abandoned, or sold out to forces, often powerful forces, of darkness. That we all are orphans, our parents too, sends each of us to loneliness, to the desert, to the search for a strong helper figure who can rescue that part of us— someone who can climb walls, who hears our call of loneliness.

Because my parents praised me so much when I was good and successful and worried so much about my sister being naughty, the wild child in me was orphaned for a long time. I was afraid to get into trouble, to take risks, to talk back. This wild part of me was locked in a tower. I always saw myself as innocent and was blind to many of the evils I did, because I could not see in the darkness of that tower. Even though I was always trying to be good, I could never feel very close to anyone. It was as if the part of me that could accept people as they are—the essence of loving—was entrapped because I could not accept all the parts of me. I was under a witch's spell. I never let my hair down to anyone—I didn't know how to.

How did I get out of that tower? By crying out, by calling out, by reaching out, by singing my song of loneliness, and letting myself be helped by those whom God has sent into my life.

There were, and continue to be, many who help my imprisoned self by calling me to let down my hair, and loving me when I let them come near. When I was very confused about my motivation for a religious life (for at thirty the reasons for entering a convent, or marrying, are not the same as at seventeen), I went for counseling to a very fine psychologist. One of the healing moments for me occurred when telling him truthfully and painfully of how I really felt inside. He said, "You are really beautiful when you are as you are now—your vulnerable self—not hiding, not pretending." He was exorcising me of the power of the witch who had kept me high in an ivory tower—pure and untouched but lonely and nonrelational.

There have been many other men and women who have been saving-prince to my imprisoned parts—who confirmed me for what I was right then—mortal and lonely. Everyone needs to be told that she is beautiful in her deepest self—the part that is often the most ambiguous and confused. The pattern of wholeness of this inner self is unique, it is hidden from her own eye and from the vision of most others.

Merton writes: "There is in all visible things an invisible fecundity, a dimmed light, a meek namelessness, a hidden wholeness. The mysterious Unity and Integrity is Wisdom, the Mother of all, *Natura Naturans* (nature naturing). There is in all things an inexhaustible sweetness and purity, a silence that is a fountain of action and of joy. It rises up in wordless gentleness and flows out to me from the unseen roots of all created being." *Hagia Sophia.* As Jesus exorcised the demons by calling them by name and bidding them leave, so it takes a human voice to call forth beauty from us.

Sometimes we like to pretend that we are not radically dependent—that we can make it alone. But if we look at life closely we see that other hands took us from the womb, and other hands will put us in the grave. Indeed, most moments of our soul's birthing and dying are by the grace of others' hands. Such is God's will for our human condition.

Perhaps you have been locked in a tower, shut up in yourself, and felt that you were calling out with no one answering. There have been times when I gave out little "peeps" and thought they were screams. Kierkegaard reminds us who often get addicted to our self-pity: "Men cry that there is no help, without having strained the understanding to find help, and afterwards they lie ungratefully."

When I am most truthful, I must confess to God and man that never have I, when locked in a tower, cried out from my heart and had that cry unanswered. When I have thought otherwise it was because I was blind to the help standing in front of me—it had too strange a face and name. My witch had blinded my eyes. I was addicted to her bitter food—to rampion.

It takes courage to be a prince willing to rescue someone crying in isolation; the witch inside that person or inherent in the circumstances may cause harm when we try to respond to another's wounded self. How often in relationships does our inner witch harm someone who is reaching out to us. We women particularly seem to turn into cats who scratch whoever is near. When we lose our beauty, our song, our long golden hair, only a true prince (or princess) has the fidelity that heals.

Rapunzel's naiveté in revealing her prince to the witch makes me ponder if somewhere, somehow, she knew that running away without confronting her wounded past would not provide ultimate release. The possibility of suffering and loss must be embraced in the spiritual journey—escaping down silken ladders is the child's way out.

Rapunzel grows from innocent, imprisoned child-girl to woman on the spiritual path of lowering, loss, separation, wounding, wilderness, and poverty. There are no spiritual short-cuts, or "bargain basement" grace, as Dietrich Bonhoeffer notes in his *The Cost of Discipleship*. The child in us somehow hopes to be exempted. The woman learns better that suffering is the way of all flesh. For the believer the suffering is redemptive, and ends in reconciliation and love. For those who will not embrace the wilderness and poverty, the suffering is a dead end.

My sister, Peggy, recently shared with me a poem she had written which was a breakthrough in accepting the sufferings of her life, not as dead ends, but as links in the chain of her story. I was deeply moved by the poem and her sharing.

These are not chains binding me
As I sometimes feel
These links are the days and years of my life—
To be added to
To be taken link by link
The strong and the weak
To complete the chain of my life.
It reminds me of the drunk who was dragging a chain
down the street.
When the policeman asked him why he was dragging
the chain,
He replied, "Have you ever tried to push a chain?"
I guess I've been trying to push my chain.

"Links of My Life" by Peggy Powell

There is terrible beauty in the final scene of the tale when the tears from Rapunzel's eyes open those of her blinded lover—tears coming from a depth and compassion made possible by the separation and wounding.

At the end of the journey of suffering freely embraced we can compassionate the collective or personal sins by which we are wounded. Jung notes:

What all should we say about that particular human being who was called mother, of whom we might even say that she was the accidental bearer of that experience which includes me and all humanity, and even all living creatures that come and go, the very experience of life whose children we are? Whatever we say will always be too much, too false, too inadequate, and even too misleading. Yet we have always done this and we shall always do it; but one who understands can no longer put such an enormous load of significance, of responsibility and duty, the weight of all heaven and hell, upon the weak and erring human being in need of love, care, understanding, and forgivenness, who was our mother. He knows that the mother is the bearer of that image inborn in us of *mater natura* and *mater spiritualis,* that image of the whole scope of life to which we are entrusted and at the same time delivered over as helpless children.[4]

I imagine Rapunzel locked in her lonely tower at first struggling bitterly with the smallness and cupidity of her parents, who turned her over to a witch through weakness and hunger for salad, hating their woundedness and hers. I know that if in the end she wept from the depths for her love, the same depths carved out by loss and wandering embraced not only her woundedness but that of her parents, of the whole world. One cannot look down on people from a heart broken through living one's humanity to the fullest. If the end of the journey is feeding on and being fed by divine compassion, perhaps the beginning of the search for the feast is our craving for earthly food, for rampion—for roots, for rampion is a root.

At a recent workshop, a woman shared with the group this poem linking her body hungers to that for God:

> *There is a hunger which no food can satisfy,*
> *And for which there is*
> *No visible means of nourishment.*
> *It is the aching of one's soul,*
> *Crying for its Mother,*
> *Pleading with its Father,*
> *To be allowed into its own home.*

"Exercising Baby" by Sara Hyatt

Now write down your responses to the story of Rapunzel making use of some of these questions if you wish:

1. What parts in you were orphaned or "sold out" by your parents?

2. Remember some occasions when you have let down your hair for someone? How did it feel? What were the results? Did some one particular person teach you how to be your simple, vulnerable self in his (her) presence?

3. Do you find it hard to let down your hair to God?

4. Remember the times you have been told you were beautiful? Did you believe the person?

5. When was the last time you told someone that he or she was beautiful? Do you find this hard to do?

6. When you are isolated, do you strain to find help? When in your life have you strained, called out loudly? How did you experience the answer? Have you, like Kierkegaard notes, ever lied ungratefully about the help that came?

7. When have you been hurt because you were trying to help someone whom you knew to be deeply isolated?

8. When have you hurt someone trying to help you?

9. When have you tried to run away from your wounded past down a silken ladder?

10. What hungers have you experienced which jolted your life, imprisoned you, and pushed you on to feed your deeper hungers?

Response to Rapunzel

RONDA CHERVIN

1. What part in you was orphaned or "sold out" by your parents? What an interesting question. My parents being both very modern and also creative tried to bring out everything they could in their daughters. But how could they bring out what they did not believe in—our souls?

I find it fascinating to think that both my twin sister and I have concentrated on the spiritual side of life with such thirst, almost always subordinating the intellectual and emotional to the exigencies of the soul. We take the life of the mind and the heart for granted. The spiritual was the forbidden fruit—the hidden rampion roots!

To some extent also the athletic side of life was orphaned. My father made attempts to get us interested in bike riding. I still recall him sacrificing long afternoons to the process of renting bikes and holding us up on them. My father loved walking and transmitted that joy to us also. But neither parent participated in any group sport. We had to learn those at camp. Mostly we did very poorly and felt mortified at being chosen last for teams.

Probably I am still smarting from the stings of peer insults when I put great energy into getting my own children into sports activities. It gives me great pleasure to see them surfing and biking. Lately I have taken up swimming and ice-skating with zest, amazed to find anything once thought unspiritual to be so refreshing.

2. The image of letting down one's hair for someone was also a favorite fairytale line for me as a child, haunting me even into adulthood.

One strange fantasy, so strong that I failed to realize at first that it was really impossible, was of myself as mother having long heavy braids down to the floor on whose ropes my babies would climb each night before bed. To such an extent did this charming image dominate my romantic ideals of motherhood that I actually grew my hair very long during my first pregnancy. I was shocked to find out that babies big enough to climb were too heavy to balance themselves on braids no matter how long.

I consider it significant that I cut off my long hair once (and never again) when my twins were a year and a half. I did not go to the beauty parlor but instead I braided my hair and then cut off the braids. It seemed symbolic of the death of the romantic image of motherhood and the resignation of becoming witch-mother.

Hair has always played an important role in my self-image. I wore my hair long throughout adolescence, and then again very long after the one big hair-chopping day of early motherhood. I wore it in a bun when trying to look older during courtship and early marriage when I wanted to match my husband's age. I put it up again for teaching but soon let it down to grow longer and longer in an attempt perhaps to be like my favorite hippie students.

Recently I let my teenage daughters cut it some four inches, during a time of discouragement. Even though almost everyone thinks the shorter (still below shoulder length) cut is more attractive, I dislike it and sometimes feel mutilated. I plan to let it grow longer and longer again. I certainly identify long loose hair with openness and vulnerability. Very often this openness and vulnerability seem threatening to others since it makes them feel their own reserve as a fault instead of a virtue. I can see more restraint can help me avoid making strangers feel invaded.

3. At first I was shy with God. I wanted to look my best—to kneel in perfect stillness—to pray the most lovely traditional prayers. Through charismatic spirituality I become more my true self in prayer and thereby experience his accepting presence as a self-evident given. He wants to love our real selves.

I wonder if the strong resistance to charismatic prayer so many religious people put up has something to do with fear of letting down their hair for God—at least in public?

4. I find it hard to believe that I am physically beautiful even when told so. I look in the mirror with a middle-aged woman's fear of the inevitable changes. I do believe that I am spiritually beautiful when I am struggling in an upward direction. When I am caught in the thistles of disgruntlement, anger, self-pity, I do not think I am spiritually beautiful. I feel this is a true estimate. Being caught in the brambles does not make us ugly if our faces are turned upward crying out for help, but we are witchlike when we refuse to cry out in pain and instead sting others with our thorns.

5. I see great beauty in others. I love to tell them about it even at the risk of embarrassing them.

6. Mary's section about seeking help when isolated and always finding it was the most moving part of her treatise for me. I became so grateful in the awareness of how many times God has sent "angels to comfort me."

7. The question about being hurt while trying to help someone known to be isolated was intriguing to me. I tend to deluge such lonely people with love. Resenting the power I might gain over

them if they admitted a need great enough to correspond to my excesses, they often do scratch out my eyes. After the pain is over I realize that I was trying to give what only God knows how to give *grace*fully, but that nonetheless my love has been needed for a time. To continue Mary's cat image—I provide a patch of sun for some alley cat. I would like this vagabond to become a purring lap-cat, but instead, when I hold too tight, the cat leaps off my lap scratching me and bounds out the window to freedom.

8. The question of how have I hurt someone trying to help me is even more painful to think about. I hate people's giving unwelcome advice according to their own life views contrary to mine when what I really want is just warmth and comfort. No doubt such helpers feel scratched when I reject their attempts to draw close for fear of their unwanted "wisdom."

In writing the last paragraph it is clear that I am guilty of the same mistake. How often I seize the opportunity of someone's melancholy to lecture them. I know I need to make an effort not to give in to this temptation, especially with my family.

9. Running away from a wounded past down silken ladders—what an image! It seems to me my whole fantasy life is just such an attempt to flee from the pain of real healing up and down romantic images of cheap paradise.

I do feel very womanly and deeply compassionate when I bear the suffering of my own existence with Christ. The joy of being resurrected tastes so much more real than the whipped cream of daydreams.

10. The hunger for *perfect* human love, truly an irrational craving, thus far continually jolts my life, making me willing to sell out everything else, yet, also pushes me toward the transcendent perfect love: God's.

Any responses or concluding images?

In a group, share you thoughts.

⚜ Hansel and Gretel

RONDA CHERVIN

My young son has a charming and slightly saccharine tape of Hansel and Gretel tracing the basic outline of this famous fairytale.

You will recall that Hansel and Gretel are the children of a poor woodcutter and an evil stepmother. This wicked woman despairs of trying to feed them all and convinces the weak father to send the children out into the forest to fend for themselves.

Overhearing their conversation, the older child, Hansel, works out a plan for circumventing the stepmother's scheme. After she has abandoned them in the forest, they will find their way home, for the clever Hansel will drop white pebbles along the path as landmarks.

This plan works the first time, but the second day he forgets to bring the pebbles and instead drops little pieces of bread which are eaten by the birds.

When Gretel realizes that they have no way to get home she begins to cry but Hansel suggests they pray to their heavenly Father for help.

Wandering around the forest they come upon a gingerbread house. This house is but the decoy of a wicked old witch who soon locks Hansel in a hen house threatening to eat him as soon as she has fattened him up. Each day he is to extend his finger so the blind witch can feel how fat he is getting.

Hansel shrewdly devises a plan. He extends a chicken bone from the slats of his prison instead of his finger so that the witch will believe him still thin.

During this time his weak little sister obeys all the witch's commands meekly, slaving for her enemy. But at the crucial moment when the witch wants her to stick her head in the big oven to light it for the cooking of Hansel, fat or thin, Gretel realizes that the witch also plans to eat her by closing the oven door on her. Suddenly Gretel becomes both shrewd and strong. She tells the witch to show her how the stove is to be lit and when the witch leans inside Gretel violently shoves her into the oven.

In the end, Hansel and Gretel take all the treasures from the house of the wicked witch and bring them back to their father's house. The evil stepmother is gone, and they live happily ever after.

When I listen to my son's tape of Hansel and Gretel, I most often focus on the poor children's being thrust out of the home and how culpable the weak father was for not preventing the exile to certain death of his own little ones.

Of course I might also identify at times with the wicked stepmother. What harried mother has not had moments when she wanted to say "Look it's them or me and they have got to go!" Fantasies of each one locked up in boarding schools dance in my tired brain . . . yielding to sentimental visions of my taking them back after the promise "to be good forever."

The feature of the story of Hansel and Gretel most intriguing however from the standpoint of *The Woman's Tale* is the way Gretel changes from the weak, tearful sister dependent first on her weak father and then on the brother who cannot save them, into the shrewd Gretel who rescues them both by shoving the witch into the oven.

Within myself I find a constant tension between wanting to be the little girl whom Daddy and older brothers will protect and deciding when they fail that I have to become shrewd and save myself and perhaps them also.

Did I think of my own father as weak or strong? My father seemed to me large and strong when I was a little girl. He was and still is rather tall and strong and healthy. He is a very independent person with strong views and little concern for what others will think of any action he takes. Since he likes to go on big and small crusades, I used to have an image of him as one above the masses doing his own thing.

I married a man twenty years older than myself, certainly in many respects a father figure. At first I planned to be completely subservient to him, work as his helpmate. During the period of his long and debilitating illness I had to become the strong one—to go out and work full-time and during his worst attacks of asthma take care of the whole load of the home duties as well. Now he is almost completely recovered and is again the staff of life for us and an invigorating companion.

I can trace in myself a pattern of seeking strong men to lean on only to find that at crucial moments they cannot help me—I must be the strong one. I am forced to learn to rely on their real strengths but not lean with all my weight, and to assume the strengths I have instead of trying to cling to still some other strong man.

After all, even our Divine Father does not shelter us from the world. "Father, I do not ask you to take them out of the world but to make them not *of* the world" (John 17:15–16).

To return to Gretel and Hansel. At first they are very afraid when they see they are lost in the forest. Then they come to the gingerbread house covered with goodies. But soon they meet the witch and realize that their dream house is full of evil.

Using the gingerbread house as a symbol of the enticing things in the world outside the original shelter, I ask myself what have I thought of at one time as a dream house which later stood revealed as containing hidden evils?

At first the church seemed to me to be a perfect house of spiritual goods, overflowing with truth, beauty, and holiness. It was quite a shock to me to realize that there was also error, mediocrity, and even terrible sin within the people in the same church: though not in its own holy essence.

At first the university where I work seemed to me a marvelous kingdom of truth and love. It was very disillusioning to realize that many, both professors and students, were bored and bitter, their motives for being there largely materialistic.

Now let us turn to the scene of Gretel under the tyranny of the witch, responding first with meekness but ultimately with shrewdness and strength. I think this scene can be used as a symbol of the situations of many women who enter the work world after being trained previously in the virtues of one-to-one personal service.

Most women, whether in low-status service jobs where meekness is highly reinforced or in executive jobs chosen for idealist reasons, think that they should cultivate openness, concern for others, and peace-making, but they are usually surrounded by at least some men who see the same situations as battlefields where aggression or shrewd manipulation is necessary for survival. Then there are always some women who by instinct or choice develop the same "masculine" battle psychology.

Many times the more "feminine" woman secretly admires masculine strategy, especially if she thinks that the goal is not personal advantage but *justice*.

This ambivalence leads to a great deal of psychological tension. Should we become as aggressive and self-seeking or assertive (in the case of just causes) as our masculine counterparts, or should we accept a certain amount of injustice or lack of success as the price for relative security and the retaining of a soft pleasing image? Should we leap in and be hard fighters or place peace and loving harmony above all else?

In my own case as a professor at a university I find myself going back and forth between aggressive attempts to win battles and then retreating from usually unsuccessful forays into a stance of "I'll just try to be a loving person and forget about these crusades."

I find it very difficult to figure out which of these two directions is the better one. I do not like the hostile person I become when I decide I am going to win at any price. I prefer the more traditionally feminine role of trying to do my best to make things loving within situations I cannot change.

I find myself with feelings of envy, fear, and rejection for those women who openly choose the "masculine" path.

Because I feel so ambivalent about this, I fail to develop the techniques of diplomatic assertiveness which might be effective in bringing about the goals I wish to achieve. But this leads often to behind-the-scenes bitterness about my fate, and also contempt for my enemies.

Gretel does not remain weak and servile; at the crucial moment she saves herself and Hansel by a violent act.

It makes me feel proud to think of times when I was strong after being weak. I picture myself driving my husband to the hospital during asthma attacks even though I was myself shaking with fear. I think of tackling a new full-time job and not giving in to moments of weakness when I would have liked to quit. I picture myself giving speeches about controversial church issues where a weaker woman would have quailed.

Thinking of these times and comparing them to times of battling unsuccessfully amidst university politics, I realize that a distinction has to be made between those times when you must be strong because something is at stake that only you can do (where being weak and fleeing to the background would be traitorous to those who need you or to the truths you stand for) and those other times when the only way to succeed would be through a type of manipulation destructive to yourself and the causes you espouse.

After the fact, it is easy to see where you had to be assertive and where you should have retreated to nurse your own and others' wounds. But how would you decide this during the fray?

Here the image of one of my favorite saints comes to mind, Teresa of Ávila. This extremely feminine Spanish lady used her charming personality for the sake of convincing people to back her up in her revolutionary endeavors, i.e., reforming convents full of chattering, compromising nuns into centers of true asceticism and contemplation. Her secret? A prayer life so deep that she could be totally convinced where God was calling her. With respect to anything that might be merely of her own devising she was ready to submit in total obedience to masculine authorities in the church. With respect to what was the will of the Lord she was given power to win over the most domineering of bishops and papal legates. The interesting thing is that she did not resort to head-on verbal collisions to prove her point. When some authority was negative to plans she was convinced were those of God, she would find some loophole, such as moving her nuns into a house far away from their original homes so that it would seem cruel for the bishop to send them back.

What would it take for me to become more like Teresa of Ávila? Obviously I would have to really have the detachment to will only what God wills and place whims and even cherished personal plans in second place. Then I would have to be willing to give myself to the dialogue with Christ with an openness allowing room for him to make his will better known. Once reasonably sure that something was right I would not rush in like a bull and stamp my foot and insist on justice, but would instead seek the most effective means of bringing it about, using all my intelligence and intuition. In this way I would be making an opening for others to see the truth instead of starting a battle of wills.

In the end Hansel and Gretel take all the treasures from the house of the wicked witch and bring them back to their father's house. The evil stepmother is gone and they live happily ever after.

In terms of *The Woman's Tale* I think that when they returned it must have been clear that Gretel was no longer just a weak little sister. She must have won equality through her saving deed. In view of my own proven strengths what kinds of equality ought I to have in the home, office, and community?

For me this question is very difficult to answer. My husband, though a greater admirer of strong, creative women, was brought up to think that women should serve in the home. A very strong character himself, he likes to make the decisions as often as possible. Since on many matters he is usually right about what to do, I find myself sinking into a pattern of going from being a leader outside the home to being Cinderella inside the home. But this frequently leads to simmering resentment. This situation is improving gradually as I become more willing to think things out in a more adult manner, retreating less and less into childish poses.

In principle, I think that both women and men should develop all their abilities in as many spheres of life as possible. Every woman should be able to take care of her car and every man should know how to change diapers and how to cook. Ideally, all decisions should be made together in consensus.

In reality, in many cases intelligent division of labor leads to a natural final decision-making role for the one who is most capable. A woman or man highly trained in education might be the natural parent to make the final decisions in a conflict about where to send the children to school. A man or woman who is an accountant might best make final decisions about the family finances. My husband is very knowledgeable about finances, purchasing, and maintenance, so he handles all these affairs, with me intervening in special cases. In general, I think that once an area of final decision-making has been carved out, it seems to me to be adolescent for a woman to insist continually on her will as a proof of equality, just as a man would be peevish who made the same claim to dominance in every area, even those about which he knows nothing. Both woman and man should try to liberate themselves from unintelligent patterns of sexist response leading to unloving behavior. For example, in our family my husband is wonderful at telling the little ones stories. Between the ages of one and a half through five the twins would sit on his lap. He would make up a new story for them every evening. I can't make up stories but I love to read to them. Right now my son has initiated a system where he reads one page and I read the next. If the woman needs a vacation alone, the man should not suddenly claim total inability to handle the household. If the man needs to go off alone the woman should not give in to childish fears of being alone at night without him.

And yet, and yet and yet—there is something repulsive to me about the image of man and woman striding forward proudly, chins up strong and independent free of all vulnerability and dependence. Equally repulsive is the image of the couple who work together spending their leisure in shrewd discourse on how to out-fox everyone else.

The last question in the following response list I almost forgot to answer because it is such a difficult one: "When have you felt that your own power as a strong woman can only come from some sort of defeat of your mother?" Notice that when Gretel returns the stepmother is gone.

In my case because my own identity crisis was resolved by becoming something totally foreign to my mother's dreams, i.e., a

Roman Catholic, the sense of coming into my own in conflict with my mother was very strong.

For many years I have rejected her strength as representing the power of everything from which I tried to escape. Often, in the struggle, I would ungratefully ignore her true virtues. I tried to be her direct opposite for a while by embracing an image of woman as receptive and supportive rather than individualistic, but I was very unhappy in this role and when I began my career I found many of the qualities of my mother, both good and bad, coming to the fore.

Your Response

Write down your response to this tale, especially regarding the character of Gretel as a typical feminine personality.

If you wish, make use of some of these questions:

1. Did your think of your own father as weak or strong when you were a child? Your mother? Trace any changes in your concept of your parents as you grew up.

2. At first the gingerbread house seems like a miracle of goodness but very soon Hansel and Gretel realize it is full of evil. In your own life can you think of environments, seemingly delightful escapes from the hardship of some previous situation, which turned out to have their own problems and evils?

3. In situations where powerful forces are aligned against your rights or advantages, do you respond with meekness or with aggression or shrewdness? When you respond strongly, do you feel you are being "unfeminine?" How do you feel about assertive or manipulative women in general and in particular?

4. Can you think of any times where you suddenly became strong when the men in your life could not help?

5. When Gretel came back to her father's house she must have seen herself as a heroine instead of a weak sister. In view of your proven strengths what kinds of equality do you think you ought to have in the home, office, and community?

6. When have you felt that your own power as a strong woman can only come from some sort of defeat of your mother?

Response to Hansel and Gretel

MARY NEILL

1. I see my father, like myself, as both weak and strong. As a little child, I always saw him as exciting and glamorous. He was away a lot or at least I was always waiting for him to return and it seemed that way to me. My sister and I used to sit on the top of the grape arbor and watch for his car to come down the road in the evening. He would come into the house and there would be activity and excitement.

My father is a tender-hearted man, and showed his feelings easily, whether of affection, or anger. I would shudder with excitement to hear him cursing at the well engine that was slow to start. (It was exciting that men could say bad things about frustrating objects, but women did not.) When he had been away a while, he always brought my sister and me a present—once a little glass train filled with candy, and another time a wonderful bear in a dome that clouded with snow when you shook it.

Later in my life I would feel some anger at him because he lacked a certain type of presence to us. He always seemed so involved in his work—he so often had to go to see a man about a job. I saw as a limitation in him that he left the rearing of the children and coloration of our minds largely to our mother. In perspective I see that he was a man of his times—struggling to support himself and us during the Depression; trained culturally to view children and religion as "women's work." I also used to consider him as not very religious.

But I have changed through the years as I have experienced how difficult it is to be a whole person and how falsely I defined spirituality. My father has faced much suffering and pain with great courage and fidelity. It moves me to see tears come to his eyes when we say blessing with all the family assembled. I am edified to feel his body praying alongside mine when we attend Mass together. In his heart and his body he believes. He asks pardon for his failings. He has remained faithful, when I am sure there are many times when he has felt like running away from the burdens of work and love.

Through a journal workshop my father emerged as a deep wisdom figure in my life—in his faith, generosity, and willingness to own his humanity.

2. When did I discover my dream house was full of evil? It really hurt me to find that in the church, in religious life, the real worldliness was deep and insidious. What the world values in a person—success, intelligence, attractiveness, good connections—are also valued in the convent. Only attractive-looking nuns served the guests. Only smart ones were sent on to study. Some sisters' parents were fussed over—others were ignored. This stunned me. There were and are so many good people in the convent that it shocked me that no one decried the subtle injuries to persons that cut deeply. Sometimes we were given talks about worldliness—i.e., strictures about being too "familiar" with seculars, about smoking or drinking intoxicating beverages. Even then I knew that there was a deeper worldliness that gnawed at the heart of the living of the Gospel; each sister was not seen or confirmed as precious in the sight of the Lord.

I never much thought that the university was a dream house, but it does shock me that so many really intelligent and powerful men and women can exercise authority and teach who have never done what I call their "emotional homework," i.e., examined the coloration of their consciousness, their prejudices. A lot of arrogance and competitiveness is accepted as common coinage and sometimes it amazes me. I always thought that everyone tried actively and consciously to become a better person in tolerance and loving kindness. It is simply not so. As Kierkegaard notes:

> No, whatever it may be that a man as a matter of course comes to, and whatever it may be that comes to a man as a matter of course—one thing it is not, namely faith and wisdom. But the thing is this: with the years man does not, spiritually understood, come to anything. And with the years one perhaps goes from the bit of passion, feeling, imagination, inwardness which one had, and goes as a matter of course under triviality's definition of understanding life.

I just did not know that intelligent and seemingly religious people could have such devotion to triviality; so little operational faith and wisdom. What causes this evil, I am not sure of in *others.* In *me,* it arises from discouragement with facing the complexity of my soul.

3. How do I fight with men or women? Not very well. I was not trained to show my anger at all, so I tend either to repress it, or dump it—neither of which is very effective. I am aware of what a disadvantage it is not to have played sports, where one learns to lose gracefully, to suit up again for the game even when discouraged, to work as a team, not to take hurts personally. I concur with the opinion I once read that women will be more effective in gaining higher jobs in business management when they have some training in the rules that men learn in sports. I get hurt too easily and I pout. I want to take my jacks and dolls and play somewhere else.

I have been working on learning to fight clean—the book, *Intimate Enemy* by J. S. Bach convinced me of its importance. My love of St. Joan of Arc assures me that I have a patroness in her. There is a time to go to war.

Once when I was struggling painfully with this incompleteness in myself, I dreamed of a Greek warrior. Greek men were trained in music, dance, poetry, sports, and war. They fought, in my imagining, nobly and cleanly. I love the story of how the Greek soldiers combed their long hair before the battle of Thermopylae. I would keep this image of the Greek warrior with me as a token from my unconscious to use when I got discouraged with fighting. Grace and skill in war can be learned and both man and woman are the better for it. It is those who think they are not violent who sometimes shed the most blood in their bludgeoning.

4. When have I had to become stronger? When I got on the plane to go and study in Europe, I had never before flown or been on a train. I had not been out of a convent-living situation for twenty years; I did not speak French; I was not yet accepted at the university, and I had no place to stay. The terror and soul-stretching which that experience required has given me courage to this day. Traveling is broadening—there are so many things you cannot control. I remember once being in Gatwick airport

with two airline tickets and no more money, being told the tickets were no good. Moments like that limber the soul. I thought at the time: "Well, I could swim the Atlantic with my suitcase in my teeth," but instead I took a nap and when I awakened, the ticket affair had sorted itself out.

5. What kinds of equality do I think I ought to have in home, office, and community?

I have no complaints about equality in the convent because we pretty much share jobs. One exception: I think that the needs of the strong ought to get equal consideration with those of the weak. I have seen frightened persons consistently insist that their minority viewpoint prevail, because they couldn't handle change. I don't think the strong should always have to give in because they are strong. Very often, too, the strong nuns do not get attention equal with the weak from the administration leaders. It is understandable why this happens—the squeaky wheel gets the oil, and so on. But cumulatively, this mindset does injustice to not only the strong but the weak. Sometimes it amounts to permission not to grow; to use one's woundedness as an excuse. Strong people need attention too. That was one of Nietzsche's great complaints about Christianity: it gave the weak too much power over the strong. There is some truth in this as I have experienced it in convent life.

At the office I would like to get equal pay with men. No women in the university—or in the United States as a whole—are paid commensurately with men. The cleavage is increasing rather than decreasing despite the affirmative action legislation. I would like my voice to carry equal weight among my colleagues in the men's club.

6. When have you felt that your own power as a strong woman could only come from some sort of defeat of your mother?

I ignored this question for a long time, yet I know that for myself and many women the separation of mother and daughter, the cutting of the psychological umbilical cord is experienced by one or the other or both as a painful "winner's/loser's" ordeal: that we hurt our mothers and say in some way, "I will no more be first of all your daughters; I will be my own person, empowered as a good woman not just from your ideals and borrowed power but by my own sufferings and achievements. I *am* my mother's daughter; I am yours—and I *am not.*" When this scene occurred in my life, I played it awkwardly and very hurtfully. Now, perhaps, I could do it better, but there is no need. I know my powers, my *self* are not borrowed from my parents. Is there a way to steal fire from the gods (even the familial ones) that does not burn us and them? I think not. All that we who believe the "Our Father" can do and must do is pray: "Forgive us our trespasses." Love for me means *always* having to say I'm sorry—despite what Eric Segal might write.

❧ Little Red Riding Hood

MARY NEILL

I dislike Little Red Riding Hood, that narcissistic little piece—in love with her own adorable red velvet cloak, who loses track of time picking flowers, who cannot tell a wolf from a grandma, who is so naive and helpless she has to be rescued, who gives clues to her own enemies to devour her with, who in the end pathetically promises her mother that she will never disobey her again, that she will always do what she is told from now on—Ugh!

The more I think about her, the more I dislike her as plain silly—a vapid woman with no depth, subtlety, nuance. What could be plumbed from the depths of a story about a shallow little girl? Freudians consider it a didactic tale whereby mothers inculcate fear of sex into their little daughters. (You will be devoured by the instinctual man—by his wolf side.) That interpretation strikes me as somewhat silly, too.

One thing I know. I can be pretty sure that anything I dismiss so sharply and cynically must speak to me of my shadow, my disowned side, so I will try to explore this dimension with you.

I like most types of women, but I really shun and discount silly women who seem to me to be preoccupied with clothes, make-up, who wander naively through wolves' territory and then howl when they get bitten. Mothers' little girls who play woodsy little games. I feel that this type of woman gets her way easily with men by accepting their instinctual projections, being all things to all men. They get terribly hurt, and they can hurt terribly. The Little Red Riding Hoods wear their weakness and naiveté on the outside and come across as charming and helpless.

I dislike them because I struggle to wear my strength on the

outside and to be very conscious and nonmanipulative in my relationships, particularly with men. I can see a wolf coming a hundred yards away, and I walk straight and cautiously through the
woods. I never, never, never would call attention to myself with a
red velvet cloak. I avoid being adorable as I would the bubonic
plague. I am the hunter who rescues others through my savvy insights into suspicious circumstances. The last thing in the world I
want to be considered is a silly, naive, helpless woman. I am an
Amazon. I consider that Red Riding Hood gives all women a bad
name.

And yet what are the despised values she contains, that I could
use to be a fuller, gentler, more human woman? She gets lost in
the tangible—the beauty of her cloak, the flowers, the curious
look of Grandma's features. She can get absorbed in details. She
trusts terribly. She is good-natured and somewhat willing to help
Grandma, but is not heavily into rescuing others. She is not really
much help—she needs help. She gets into trouble.

I really need some of these qualities—sticking to specifics, instead of always seeing the forest. Getting lost in details has a
gift—a contemplative aspect. I'm too goal-oriented and don't
enjoy enough the path—the getting there. Catherine of Siena
says, "All the way to heaven is heaven, for He has said, 'I am the
Way.' " I rarely experience that because my head would be full of
Grandma and I wouldn't see the flowers for the task. I need to
trust beautiful clothes, the feel of fabrics; to trust strange forms
that life can take. I need to accept people's disguises more; not be
so suspicious. In every Grandma, I look for a wolf and sometimes
it is just a Grandma, unsettled by my suspicion.

I need to let myself get swallowed up sometime and know I can
survive. I am pretty cautious about relationships. I make sure that
I don't get eaten up—maybe too sure.

I know it sounds strange, but I can see that silliness has its
place, too. I get so deadly serious about my rescue/helping roles,
about my inner life and its wounds, about my work and its perils.
I'm even serious about playing! This makes me plenty intense and
high-powered around people. I know that I make them and myself uncomfortable at times with this intensity. A little silliness
gives people more space. My getting a little lost (or just showing

my lostness) would let them be finders/keepers instead of the losers/weepers I must help.

We too seldom reflect, we strong women, that it is good to let our weak-woman part show, to give another the opportunity to save us. St. Thomas Aquinas makes it clear that he who gives has more benefit than he who receives. So we "givers" need to own our greediness. Our shadow is the wolf who preys on the weakness of others, using their weakness to make ourselves feel strong in comparison. We who follow Christ know the ideal of kenosis—of emptying, he calls us to, who did not cling to being God, but emptied himself, taking the form of a slave. And "God has chosen the foolish of this world to confound the wise." How ironic for me who has lived the Amazon woman, the Joan of Arc, if I find that the little Red Riding Hoods have made it to greener mansions than mine in heaven. But I know that the Lord is full of surprises, that he confounds the proud and exalts the lowly; the rich he sends empty away. One of the terrible temptations for those who have sloughed long and hard on the spiritual trail is that of pride—a kind of sureness that we know what the Lord likes; that he likes my type of woman—not silly women.

But this notion is my profound silliness, outweighing that of all Red Riding Hoods: that I think I know the mind of the Lord, that I will exclude from his compassion and understanding what I exclude from mine—silly women. Wasn't it silly for the mother of James and John to ask for the best seats in the kingdom for her sons? Yet Jesus called her to be at the foot of his cross. Wasn't it silly of Mary Magdalene to waste all that perfume and break the jar, to sob in public and wipe his feet with her hair? Even silly women can love; can be loved.

Response

Write your own self-exploration of Red Riding Hood. Some questions to ponder:

1. What fairytale character do you actively dislike? What does it reveal to you of your shadow? Of your unlived life? Of despised values?

2. What kind of silliness do you see in yourself and other women? How do you deal with it?

3. What is the wolf in you? What is your strength that needs other's weakness for its food?

4. Do you ever consciously try to minimize your own strength so as not to deplete others?

5. Do you let others rescue you? Why? Why not? Write down any memories you have of rescue operations and your role in them.

Response to Little Red Riding Hood

RONDA CHERVIN

Reading Mary's account of Red Riding Hood brought many images to mind. People used to nickname me Red Riding Hood for the five years or so when I wore a bright red raincoat spring, summer, and fall. In children's plays I also often played that role.

On a psychological plane I found myself identifying in some ways with Mary's description of Red Riding Hood's faults. Though too serious to be silly, I tend to act naive and girlish with older men in the perennial search for fatherly love. This works out well except that it undermines any attempts to achieve intellectual or spiritual equality with such men. Situations involving groups of men such as department meetings with both older and fatherly men and with others young or competitive throw me, as I try to combine the image of the crusading Joan of Arc with that of the charming little Red Riding Hood in need of protection. No wonder I find such situations tense!

The "wolf" image is ambivalent for me. On the one hand I am attracted by the wolf type. I would like to be devoured by some powerful male. On the other hand the wolf type seldom likes me. Even in my pre-Christian days of sexual liberation I was never able to relax into sensuality—I always felt more on my own grounds with conversation and argument.

There is a woman I know who fits Mary's description of the sweet adorable naive type very well. I find myself cherishing her charm and her relaxed oneness with nature—yet this affirmation of her is mingled with envy which often takes the form of trying to push her into being more self-confronting. After pondering Mary's ideas I am inclined to think my treatment of her is harsh and that I should just enjoy her as a very special creature of God and not insist that she take on the burden of my self-styled authenticity.

To respond to the other questions:

What fairytale girl do I hate? The little Mermaid! This is a story involving a mermaid who sacrifices herself completely unto death for her prince. I hate this story so much that I have blocked out the narrative. My dislike of the story probably reflects a deep fear of so surrendering to some male as to allow myself to be annihilated—an interesting contrast to the desire to be swallowed by the wolf mentioned earlier.

I wonder if this fear operates as an obstacle to complete surrender to the Christ who does thrust before us an image of total self-immolation, though, of course, with a certain Resurrection.

Your additional ideas?

⚜ Beauty and the Beast

RONDA CHERVIN

Once there was a rich merchant who had six children, three boys and three girls. All the girls were beautiful but the youngest was the most admired, so much so that everyone called her Beauty—which made the others jealous. The older girls were proud in their wealth and sought rich husbands. The youngest girl enjoyed staying home and reading and keeping her father company.

Then suddenly the father lost his money and the family had to move to a poor cottage in the forest. The older sisters were wretched; bored to death, they spent the days lamenting the loss of their party life. But Beauty flourished. She did all the household chores and then spent time reading, playing her harpsichord, or singing at her spinning wheel.

Then after a year's time the father got news of one of his ship's coming successfully into port. He left with the promise to bring back all sorts of frippery for the older girls, but Beauty when pressed asked only for a single rose.

On the way home from his unsuccessful trip to town, the father got lost in a snow drift. Finally he saw a large house in the distance. Inside there was a fine table covered with good things to eat. He waited to see who would come but finally when no one did, he ate the whole dinner and went to bed. The next day he plucked a rose for Beauty and started out for home only to be stopped by a horrible Beast.

The Beast told the man that he would eat him unless he sent back a daughter to die in his place. The man agreed, determined *not* to sacrifice a daughter but at least to see his family again before dying.

Once he was home, Beauty insisted on his daughter accompanying him back to the castle of the beast so that at the last minute she could take her father's place. But before they take off, Beauty has a dream in which a lady comforts her with the words: "I am pleased with your kind heart, Beauty; the good deed you are doing by sacrificing your life to save your father's will not go unrewarded."

Instead of eating her, the Beast showered her with gifts. By and by she realized that even though the Beast is ugly he has a kind heart and finally Beauty ceases to see him as ugly. But when he asks her if she will be his wife she refuses.

She promises to stay and be his friend, however, begging only for one last visit to see her father. The Beast agrees, but on condition that she return in eight days, otherwise he will die of grief.

Beauty returns to her home, but though her sisters are now married to witty and rich men, they are still consumed with jealousy and they plot to keep her from returning after the eight days so that the Beast might punish her. They succeed with a trick in retaining her past the promised eight-day limit.

Beauty dreams that the Beast is dying of grief and so decides after ten days that she must return and marry him. She goes back to the castle, but after searching all over she cannot find the Beast. Finally she finds him half dead in the garden. She begs forgiveness of him for staying away so long and promises to marry him.

Upon hearing those words the Beast changes into a handsome prince. He explains that he had been enchanted and had to stay in the form of a beast until a beautiful girl would consent to marry him.

The good fairy comes and tells Beauty that since she preferred virtue over handsomeness and wit she deserves to find all three united in one person: the wonderful prince.

The fairy then turns the jealous sisters into stone statues with no other punishment than to witness Beauty's happiness. They can return to being human only when they admit their faults.

In my family I felt myself to be like Beauty—the admired one, and at the same time the one who could be very content cooking, playing solitaire, reading. At school it was the opposite—I was the envious one looking at the more sophisticated, richer girls with mournful longing.

The "rose" represents for me different crosses to wear around my neck. Usually these have been gifts—often from my [non-Catholic] husband—which makes them especially touching. I usually wear them until they fall off my neck—I wear them to bed, in the shower, and always showing above my clothing because being a lover of Christ is important to my identity.

Like the Beast, I sometimes bribe people with extravagant love, praise, and adoration—the exorbitant demand at the end being that they should "be my best friend forever" and be willing to absorb the passionate love energy I want to give them. Like the Beast I threaten to die if they leave me and they usually do! Then I curl up and play dead, as it were, until I spy another prospect on the horizon.

I would and do sacrifice my life for my children and husband in a daily way. Recommitment after bouts of resentment always leads to unexpected forms of family happiness.

Some amusing examples come to mind—rushing out to spank a child and suddenly instead mid-grasp starting to laugh and hug that child. I think of such transformations of anger to joy as illustrating a recurrent pattern from the lives of different saints where they would kiss a leper or a poor beggar and the leper would become Christ.

Very often it is the students I teach who seem like lepers to me when they become unresponsive and hostile and yet I must go into that lion's den and kiss them symbolically. If I continue to be frightened of them they become more hostile. I can only break the ice by loving them more than before. I am sure that "kissing the beast" so that he becomes a prince is deeply related to forgiveness and hence comes very close to the essence of Christianity. In fact, the willingness to move out freshly is a sign that inner forgiveness has taken place.

Sometimes the beast who becomes a prince when kissed is my

literary work. I start out with a shining idea that suddenly by evil enchantment becomes a cumbersome beast. I flee, promising to return. I am seduced by more pleasing prospects. I can only return to my project by first "forgiving" it for being so recalcitrant. But if I am willing to come back and swear fidelity to it, often my typewriter becomes winged and my words fly out swiftly in spite of previous obstacles.

Is there right now some virtuous path I shun carrying with it the possibility of new happiness? Yes. I think the leper I must kiss is life itself with all its changes and disappointments. I must kiss the hands of God and receive his gift and not whine that it does not look like the prince I wanted. I think of the Virgin Mary, who must have dreamed of being the mother of the Messiah, but found herself the mother not of the glorious King of Kings on earth but rather of one shunned and persecuted. The King of Kings emerged from the total sacrifice.

Your Response

You may like to write response to this story or answer any of the following questions if they provoke you to inner dialogue:

1. In your own family or at school did you feel that you were more like the older sisters or like Beauty—the admired one?

2. Were you ever perfectly content doing menial chores or enjoying solitary recreations?

3. What in your life represents the rose—something inexpensive but treasured as a symbol?

4. Do you ever bribe people as the Beast did with his fine dinners, only to make extreme demands on them afterward?

5. For whom or for what would you be willing to sacrifice your life?

6. Go through your life-tale and think of times when you have had to make a commitment against your wishes to someone or some job that seemed repulsive to you, and that resulted in unexpected happiness afterward?

7. Is there some virtuous path you shun right now that might possibly bring happiness?

Response to Beauty and the Beast

MARY NEILL

I find it easy to identify with some aspects of Beauty. In my early years I worked hard at pleasing others; both at school and at home so I would be praised, so that I would be considered, if not physically beautiful, at least beautifully behaved. I was content to do all my chores and lessons. I was never a demanding child. Dad always brought us a present when he came home. I do not ever remember asking for anything in particular.

These qualities, I see now, came not from a genuine inner beauty but from a desire to be considered a beautiful good girl— to be special, to be praised. This addiction to being thought well of stands today as an obstacle at times to my endurance of certain inevitable conflicts in my work and home life.

Coloring oneself to enhance one's environmental self may be pleasing for a while but the virtue and praise it brings are but skin deep. I never felt a deep inner beauty. Once, however, I dreamed of a dark-haired sleeping beauty and could own that she was there somewhere in my depths.

The spiritual task for me has been to leave my father's house (my environmentally shaped notions of pleasing others and of seeming beautiful to them) and learn to live with and confront the Beast within me—the unloved shadow parts. Because I have been basically a good, biddable girl, it has taken me a long time to own my genuine capacity for evil—to see that it is a negative beast—deformed, unpleasing, bound under a spell of rejection and sadness. This beast in me has been so unloved it threatens to die at each rejection; it bribes others and terrifies them with its neediness.

I have come to see that I served others' needs so earnestly because my inner beast was so needy. But I could not show that neediness, that emptiness to others, lest I die from their rejection. Neediness seemed ugly—at least it felt ugly.

We so hate to be needy because of that feeling of rawness; it presses us to ugly demands on ourselves and others. How we crave the nurturing confirmation of that part of us by someone, by anyone, but we do not show it, and so the split widens between our environmental self and our deeper self hidden in Christ, the same Christ who was "despised whereupon we esteemed him not; whose countenance was as it were hidden. Yet he was beautiful among the sons of men, and by his bruises we are healed" (Isaiah 53:3).

The beginning of Mark's Gospel tells us that the spirit led Jesus to the desert where he lived amid the wild beasts. Jesus was not only the lamb of God, but the lion of Judah, the second Adam, who like the first had power to call all beasts by their name, ordering them in the new Eden. Through Christ's grace, I have been given courage and help to name my beastly side—to see that I am not such a beautifully behaved girl—or woman, and that is all right, too. I am like Christ's friend Peter—mortal, faltering in good; wavering in faith, wounded and wounding with original and personal sin—yet that mortal flesh is what God embraced in Christ, redeemed and loved, found and still finds beautiful.

It is freeing to know that I do not have to be "Our tainted nature's solitary boast" (Wordsworth) in order to be beautiful in God's eyes. The more I become aware of my inner beauty (not as the world sees it, but as Christ sees it) the more beauty I see around me. Working with my dreams and in my journal has been most helpful in giving me new perspective. As Emily Brontë writes in *Wuthering Heights:* "I've dreamt in my life dreams that have stayed with me ever after, and changed my ideas; they've gone through and through me, like wine through water, and altered the colour of my mind" (quoted in John Sanford's *Healing and Wholeness,* pp. 148 ff.).

I have dreamed dreams and found images of hope and beauty, absurd perhaps to others, that have helped me see beauty anew. One of the really important dreams of my life has been this one.

I am walking through a beautiful old Victorian house, full of plants and people and polished floors. I realize that I do not belong in this house, though it is comfortable. I go through the back door and meet there in the garden a friend deeply loved, yet from whom I am deeply divided. He gives me flowers and I know that we will be reconciled. Then I am walking along the ocean shore and I look up at the sky and see the Southern Cross. I think: "Ah,

I have come to the Southern Hemisphere." The cross seems a diamond pendant and it moves from the sky into my heart. I awake with a deep feeling of ecstasy.

Beauty, as you remember, had two dreams that guide her way. Whenever I get discouraged with the trials and complexities of my life—the ugliness within and without—I think of the beauty of this dream—the courage to know what is not one's home; the beauty of flowers and reconciled love—the at-one-ment of the cross that turns me around and presses into my heart, drawing me to peace.

I do not mean to give the impression as if all is beauty; that there is no beast left in me to kiss; as if the inner marriage has been consummated. It has and it has not. My mind sees the cross in the sky, but my heart is addicted to hurting, hiding division. It has experienced the single rose of God's taming love, yet still answers to the call of the wild beast within. I just am scared of being tamed by God, truth to tell. Burned by the fires of environmental taming, I fear the greatest chastening bond of all. "Yet I, except you enslave me, never shall be free/nor ever chaste, except you ravish me" (John Donne).

Responses, Images, Sharings? Put them in your notebook.

⚜ Sleeping Beauty

MARY NEILL

Sleeping Beauty," or Briar Rose, has a subtle fascination for me, though it is a very simple, almost abstract fairytale. I put off writing about it for a long time and twice fell asleep after picking up my pen to unpack its energy. Though I like to think of myself as a wide-awake, swiftly moving, and growing person, I have to acknowledge that from reflection even on the way I approach this tale, something in me still slumbers, bonded under a drowsy curse. I would like to think that what is slumbering is insignificant, but I suspect it is not.

The story of Sleeping Beauty, you will remember, concerns the birth of a beautiful girl to a king and queen who have waited long sterile years for a child. At the great celebration of her birth they invite not only friends and relatives but all wise women (godmothers) who are kind and affectionate to children. There are thirteen such women in the kingdom, and the king has only twelve golden plates, so one such woman has to stay home. At the culmination of the feast, the wise women present their gifts—virtue, riches, beauty, and so on—and then suddenly the thirteenth woman, not invited and jealous, curses the child with death.

Luckily one blessing remains. The last wise woman says that at the age of fifteen, when Rose will prick her finger on a spindle, she will fall into a deep sleep for one hundred years. The king does everything possible to protect Rose from having contact with a spindle, but on her fifteenth birthday, her parents are away and she finds in a hidden room of the castle a woman spinning. Curiosity prompts her to touch the spindle. After pricking her finger she falls into a deep sleep, and the sleep spreads throughout the castle. The horses in the stables, the doves under the eaves, the flies upon the wall, and even the fire upon the hearth, all cease to stir. Even the wind ceases to blow. A thick hedge of brairs grows over the castle and brings death to many young men who get lost in the thickets.

A fearless young prince, hearing the legend one hundred years later, braves death from the hedge, and its thorns turn to flowers as he passes. He sees the arrested life throughout the castle, finds the beauty sleeping, and kisses her awake. All life starts again. They marry and live happily ever after.

How simple this tale is—birth, blessing, curse, sleep, rescue. It is a wonderful fairytale to act out with young children. I remember being a substitute mother for three weeks to three children aged seven, nine, and eleven, and enacting with them many times the awakening scene—sometimes tenderly, sometimes hilariously, as they made up their own scripts and switched parts endlessly. If "I once was lost and now I'm found" reflects a profound experience of the soul's journey, so must: "I once was cursed and asleep and now I am awake and loved."

That is what the name Buddha means: "I am awake." He saw most men as sleep-walking, avoiding the hard path to enlightenment. I find it really hard to work to become fully conscious; it is painful and separating. The more light I shed on my myself inside, the more woundedness and sinfulness I see. I like to imagine that deliverance is all from within, within my own power; that I can shed the light where I will and be delivered, but experience and my faith tell me that do what I may, both the curses and blessings from my birth come through others and so does my deliverance.

It has been really hard for me to accept that there is always a curse as well as a blessing at all beginnings—that this is the way of all flesh. Birth and new life are given—yes often after long years of sterile waiting—but there is always the shadow, the part inside you or outside (left out and overlooked, rejected and unfed) that comes to take its revenge. In my rearing and life choice, the shadow came to be carried by any powerful or dangerous or negative feelings—anger, fear, or sexual. These were not invited to be a part of my life and so were left neglected, unowned, disowned, unclaimed. But because their neglect has been a curse and they are the life force from God moving to new life—especially the sexual feelings—they have time and again pushed through, asking to be removed from the shadow's curse.

Nancy Friday's book *My Mother, Myself* suggests that for many women there is a curse, inherited through generations, which encourages us to remain ignorant about our bodies. We hope that if one just does not know or look at something, especially something powerful and ambivalent, it will go away. One chooses sleep and unconsciousness, and so our life energy is frozen, halted, blocked. Our energies are imploded. John Layard writes in *The Virgin Archetype:* "There is nothing in nature that is not there in order to be transformed and it is a universal phenomenon that the 'natural' which always starts by being good becomes regarded as bad if or when it does not submit to transformation" (p. 264). And he warns: "Sexual repression hinders spiritual development because it is not available for transformation" (*ibid.*). It takes courage to let ourself experience dangerous or negative feelings, or even very powerful positive feelings. Yet we know that Jesus must have experienced all that each human does; that energy flowed powerfully through him and from him; that he was a transformer and calls us to be one also.

Which of your life energies lies under a curse?

The wounding of Briar Rose at the spindle, that feminine instrument so often associated with the spinning of fate, reminds me of the shadow side of my own spinster feminine—the old woman locked away in an inaccessible room who continues to spin, contrary to the laws of the kingdom. I spin many things in locked-away rooms—fears, fantasies, projections, tales about others. We women often spin webs for ourselves and others that cause profound injury or loss. I spin reasons for my enmities, for rejection, for discounting myself that rob me and others of beauty; that freezes life between us.

Again Nancy Friday points out how competitive and cruel women can be to one another, spinning reasons for rejecting. She feels that we are raised in a kind of subtle competitiveness for love and praise—in an economy of scarcity; as if there were not enough love or praise to go around. How does the "spinster" in you work for good and evil? Do you feel that there is enough love and praise to go around? If not, why not? If yes, when did the consciousness of plenty begin for you? (Nancy Friday writes: "When we were little, we had to live by mother's rules. It was her house, her man. Now there are enough men to go around, and the rules are up to us. If we lose one job to another woman, there is another good one around the corner. Fear of competition is nurtured by notions of living in a psychic economy of scarcity. Grown up life is an economy of abundance" [*My Mother, Myself,* p. 201].)

The image of frozen time—the details of the cessation of movement—are all very poignant for me. I was deeply moved when I saw the "frozen" city of Pompeii ten years ago—the outline of a dog, some bread, some eggs. I knew this must speak to some image locked in my soul—bits of life frozen in time, unused, waiting to move. "Shall these dry bones live?" asks Jeremiah and the Lord says yes. Different friends in my life have breathed spirit into frozen parts. My sense of humor was reawakened by one friend in particular. My joy in dancing and good films by another. The beauty of the Bible by another.

"Look at that," says our mother to us as children, unfreezing some object hidden in a cluttered environment, and ever after, love and life and movement come from some prince of a person who kisses awake, who breathes into a sleeping part. I had always wanted to write a book but that notion remained frozen until Ronda breathed life and possibility into me. Ira Progoff breathed spirit into another sleeping skill—journal writing and teaching. So many are the gifts the spirit has breathed awake in me through others' inspiration—"in-breathing." What gifts have been breathed to life in you by other's breath? their confirmation, inspiration, encouragement, love? Which still lie dormant, waiting life?

The last image that strikes me in the tale is that of the briars that grow about the castle to keep others out. How many times I have impaled others on my thorns, when I was really crying to be released. How grateful I have been to those courageous enough to risk injury to get to the beauty locked within. What are your thorns which turn people away? Whose hands have turned the thorns to roses? How willing are you to risk injury in order to help unlock some sleeping beauty in others?

Just as it was hard to address this fairytale, so it is hard to leave it. Something still sleeps in me, still waits—beyond the words I can say. The music of the Gregorian plain chant excerpt from the "Song of Songs" says it for me—a little. *"Ego dormio et cor meum vigilat—aperi mihi, soror mea, columba mea, immaculata mea."* "I sleep and my heart watches. Open to me my sister, my dove, my spotless one." Christ speaks to each soul, calling it to awaken to love. Yet so often we sleep on, believing more in ancient curses than in the prince that comes, ever nearer.

Wallace Stevens's poem, "The World as Meditation" describing Penelope spinning, guarding her beauty, longing for deliverance by her lover, evokes, too, a little of what my words cannot touch.

She wanted nothing he could not bring her by coming alone.
She wanted no fetchings. His arms would be her necklace
And her belt, the final fortune of their desire.
But was it Ulysses? Or was it only the warmth of the sun
On her pillow? The thought kept beating in her like her heart.
The two kept beating together. It was only day.
It was Ulysses and it was not. Yet they had met,
Friend and dear friend and a planet's encouragement.
The barbarous strength within her would never fail.
She would talk a little to herself as she combed her hair,
Repeating his name with its patient syllables,
Never forgetting him that kept coming constantly so near.

Listen to some music or find some poetry that speaks to your sleeping, waiting beauty—whose eyes are closed, who has no words.

Your Response

What does the image of Sleeping Beauty mean to you? Write about it. Here are some questions.

1. Has it been hard for you to see, to accept, that there is both a curse and a blessing involved in all beginnings?

2. What parts of your life have been neglected, unowned, disowned, unclaimed?

3. Which of your life energies lies under a curse?

4. What is the shadow side of your spinning of tales?

5. How does the "spinster" in you work for good and evil?

6. Do you feel that there is enough love and praise to go around? If not, why not? If yes, when did the consciousness of plenty begin for you?

7. What gifts have been breathed into life in you by another's breath—their inspiration, confirmation, encouragement, love?

8. Which parts of you lie frozen, awaiting life?

9. What are the thorns in you which turn people away? Whose hands have turned the thorns to roses? (Or have you thought to do this on your own?)

10. How willing are you to risk injury in order to help unlock some beauty sleeping in others?

11. Listen to some music or find some poetry that speaks to your sleeping, waiting beauty; whose eyes are closed, who has no words.

Response to Sleeping Beauty

RONDA CHERVIN

Here again the imagery of Mary's analysis evokes so many hidden feelings: something still slumbering, bonded under drowsy curses!

What are my cursed energies? Mostly physical ones. I have always been clumsy, somewhat weak, and easily tired. And yet I hate the image of weakness and so will do some physical things on a dare—like running into the ocean no matter how cold, or diving, or skating, or driving fast.

But these are all things involving movement. What is really cursed is the sensual as a state of relaxed enjoyment. Such sensuality as lying in the sun, lounging in a hot tub, stroking people to a degree that seems neurotic rather than justifiable.

The image of the "spinster spinning webs of envy" was very sharp. I feel disgusted with myself when I give in to the urge to sit with other women in our own "hidden room" and gossip. The idea that such envy springs from fear that there is not enough praise to go around is telling. The resentment that my daughters were princesses and I a drudge was relieved by the birth of my son who balanced things so nicely by loving each person in the family with such extravagant affectionate joyfulness.

Frozen parts brought to life by a kiss? Friends encouraging me to write freely instead of academically; children making me laugh; my sister, the dancer, inspiring me to dance too; Mary Neill evoking courage to face Crosses without flight.

Thorns turning people away? I sometimes try to annihilate people who make me feel insecure by devastating arguments against their philosophies of life.

Music speaks deeply to my sleeping lyricism. I love the music of Delius with its heavy-scented flowing melodies.

Your reflections?

⚜ Woman Deserted: Solveig, Gretchen, and Regina

RONDA CHERVIN

There are three women in literature and history I identify with for the same reason—they represent *women deserted.*

I would guess that many of you do not know who these women are because they figure simply as the victims of the famous men who loved and left them: Solveig, the bride of Peer Gynt of the Ibsen play and Grieg music; Gretchen or Marguerite of Goethe's masterpiece Faust; and Regina, the fiancée of Kierkegaard, the Danish philosopher-theologian.

Let me summarize their tales briefly.

Peer Gynt, the adventurer, falls deeply in love with the beautiful maiden Solveig. They consummate their love, but Peer leaves suddenly to escape from entanglements of past misdeeds, promising to return. The faithful Solveig awaits his return with sad hopefulness. He returns many years later after having forgotten her completely.

Faust, the middle-aged professor, makes a pact with the Devil, selling his soul for renewal of youth and the conquest of the innocent young Gretchen. After seducing her, he abandons her, pregnant and shamed, to the mercy of the people of her village. Accused of murdering her mother, to whom she had given a sleeping potion on the night of the seduction, she is imprisoned and goes insane. In the final scene she is forgiven by God and pleads successfully for redemption for Faust, whose soul is snatched from the hands of the Devil at the last moment.

Regina was a young girl who won the heart of the sophisticated and brilliant Sören Kierkegaard. Although he truly loved his fiancée, Kirkegaard suddenly broke the engagement for reasons arising from a melancholy fear of a death curse on his family, a morbid introspective disposition, and a sense that he was meant to be a celibate even though such a choice had no place in his Danish Lutheran church. Though genuinely heart-broken after the breaking of her engagement, Regina finally recovered, married another man, and raised many children very happily.

Until sitting down to write this piece it had never occurred to me that this theme must be universal. I wanted to write about it primarily to try to see if analysis could help quiet the pain of facing the recurrence of a pattern I can trace all the way back to childhood.

When my father left on a sales trip and came home only briefly to announce that he was going to marry someone else, my twin sister and I were stunned. We, at eight, did not really comprehend what was happening. We had never even heard the word "divorce" before. Our parents had never fought, for they had psychological theories against children being let in on parental conflicts.

In retrospect it seems to me that I repressed the pain of this separation pretty well. I had always been closer to my mother than to my father, and this provided an occasion for even deeper intimacy since I became my mother's solace and main companion. It was only later on, when I had married a man who was a sales manager, that I realized how deep that wound had gone, for whenever my husband went on a sales trip, in spite of his great love for me, I became convinced that he would never return. Also, since the sixteen-year-old daughter of my father's second wife seemed to us gangly eight-year-olds to be the height of sexy sophistication, I find that I tended to think of myself as unattractive and would become morbidly jealous of any older, more poised, woman—sure that such a one would rob me of any man I might love. I viewed all men as Peer Gynts, who might love me fervently but could leave me suddenly and not return.

In my youthful love relationships, although many a time it was I who did the rejecting, in the cases where I was the one to be abandoned the scenario would often run painfully along the same lines—happiness in love followed by an inexplicable break-up.

My reactions would follow a pattern of suicidal anguish, long-ing sadness, feeling utterly crushed, and then being buoyed up by some new enthusiasm. In most cases I would not become resentful or bitter, but neither would I come to the point of forgivenes. It is more as if I turned against myself as too unlovable to be a recipi-ent of faithful love.

And yet I can find explanations for why men leave women—ex-planations having nothing to do with the woman. I can under-stand fathers leaving their children—young men falling madly in love with a girl but wanting something else more at the moment, such as success in a career; older men becoming desperate seeking distraction from the maturity demanded of family life, etc. etc.

What good comes from being a deserted woman? My first re-sponse to my own question would be a cry of pain—nothing good at all—only unbearable sadness. But really this is only a part of the truth—and only a very little part. In many ways the rejections by men have thrown me back on my own resources. Because I had no man to idol-worship who would utterly cherish me in such a secondary role, I was forced to become my own person. I had to come to grips with inner solitude, singing my own songs like Solveig.

Like Gretchen, the disillusionment with the Fausts in my life led me finally to cling to a Divine Savior—one whose love never fails. Anguish that all things human were so transitory brought me into a much deeper, more emotional and mystical type of reli-gious life than a life of greater contentment might have done.

Finally, like Regina, here I am happily married, surrounded by dear children, leading a full rich life. From the heart of pain comes compassion. In eternity God will wipe away all our tears. And not only in eternity—since the writing of this book my hus-band has decided to become a Catholic. This has opened up a new level of sharing, not only on a spiritual but also on an emo-tional level, to a degree I never thought possible. Alleluia!

Your Response

In what ways would you, the reader, identify with any of these women's tales? Write a free-style answer or respond to some of the questions listed here:

1. Have there been times in your life when some beloved masculine figure has left unexpectedly? No matter how painful, write a description of these incidents.

2. What was your reaction to being left behind? Sadness? Longing? Rage? Resentment? Forgiveness? Bitterness?

3. Can you trace reasons why each man might have left you in terms of *his* tale?

4. What good can you see coming from these rejections?

Response to Woman Deserted

MARY NEILL

The woman deserted is a poignant image at all times and particularly when so many women find themselves divorced and alone, unsalaried and unskilled.

I suppose one of the "perks" of religious life is that one is protected from the shattering loss of a bond into which one has poured long years and much energy. The pain I felt at one rejection was so great that I can only imagine what it must be where there has been a major life and energy investment.

I can remember walking through the hills for two or three days with a young woman friend who had been rejected by someone she loved deeply. She could not even talk—so numb she was with pain. I said, "Be mad at him." But she could not—she loved him and he had been just in breaking off. Maybe it is easier when one is treated unjustly.

Again I remember the pain of a friend whose fiancé had called off the wedding two weeks before the ceremony. We women forget how many more rejections men must face, because societal roles often demand that they be the initiator and risk rejection. Also, the number of people who hate themselves for years after a divorce seems to be as "numberless as the stars" in our times.

When I am feeling rejection, I try to take it now as a challenge not to reject myself—not to be a sea anemone that lives only by instinctual opening and closing. I have at times listed all the occasions when I have felt rejected and then dialogued with rejection itself, as if it were a person, a tough enemy with whom I must combat and demand my due. I have asked over and over and have prayed to know: "What is the gift that rejection has to give?" This, the shadow that follows all relationships.

Kierkegaard, who rejected Regina, noted wisely that we in loving try to give ourselves away, especially in our "poetic" loves. When the relationship ends, we despair because we are given ourselves back to love ourselves, "Alone again, naturally," as the song goes. The transcendent leap—the leap of faith demanded—is then to will to be oneself alone, transparently grounded in God. But this leap is not a trick—it is rather the long night journey across the sea, ten thousand fathoms deep.

This learning to get the gift from rejection strengthens us for the last ultimate rejection—death—when life itself seems to cast us aside. Be we so special—a Beethoven, a Buddha, the Christ—we are given over to death—a large rejection indeed, beside which all smaller rejections seem hors d'oeuvres. If, as Emily Dickinson wrote, each parting is a little death, so too is each rejection. Learning to keep faith in oneself, in life, in love, in the face of rejection is to grow in the deep faith that we are loved ultimately by the father of life—that we are just not rear-guard troops called to the fore when others die, only to be turned in for new battalions. Our faith is that of Jesus—that we can call in the darkness "Abba, Father," and that, "Eye has not seen nor ear heard what God has prepared for those who love him."

1. Write down the memory of the most painful rejection you've ever suffered. Can you see its gift?

2. Remember when you rejected someone? Would you handle it differently now?

⚜ Amor and Psyche

MARY NEILL

A *mor and Psyche* is the most complex of the stories considered
here. First written by the Roman Apuleius at the beginning
of the Christian era, it is often considered as a pattern of the heroine's courageous inner journey. Many explications of it are
around now, for example, Erich Neuman's *Amor and Psyche*, Robert Johnson's *She,* and C. S. Lewis's *Til We Have Faces.* I am inclined to the opinion that it speaks not just of the woman's journey, but of the soul's journey, for that is what the Greek word *psyche* means. (I have a sense that the myth of the woman's journey
per se has yet to be written because it is just now being lived by all
those women seeking their deepest self unfolding before God and
man in these hyperconscious times.)

The story goes like this. Psyche, one of three daughters born to
a king and queen, is so beautiful that mortals become forgetful of
the goddess of love Aphrodite, who takes revenge against her. Psyche is sentenced to be thrown from a cliff, but Aphrodite's son,
Eros, falls in love with her and wafts her away to a castle where he
visits her by night, never revealing his face. Although she is very
happy, she longs to return home to see her sisters and so Eros re-
luctantly agrees. The sisters press her for details about her husband and when her floundering replies reveal the unusual
arrangements, they suggest that he is a serpent who will kill her
and the child she is expecting.

Armed with a knife and a lamp, Psyche is ready to kill her
nightly lover, but instead when the light reveals his beauty, she is
stricken with a profound love. She drops oil on his shoulder and
he wakes and flees, wounded.

Psyche is heart-broken and near suicide, searching for him. At length she comes to his mother, her arch-rival, who berates her and gives her four arduous near impossible tasks to complete if ever she is to find her love again.

On the first day she is to sort thousands of varied seeds. When Psyche sobs, helpless, the ants come to help her sort out the mass of detail.

Next Psyche is told to get some of the golden fleece from the fierce rams on the Isle of the Sun. A water reed advises her to wait until nightfall and collect the fleece that clings to the bushes rather than risk facing the rams head-on.

Her third task is to take a small crystal vase and fill it with the water of life, which falls from the tall crags into the depth of the earth, with never an accessible foothold near. This time an eagle saves Psyche by flying to the crag and filling the vase for her.

The most arduous task is the last: to travel to the underworld to bring back beauty in a box from Persephone, the queen there. A tower warns Psyche that she must take two coins in her mouth for crossing the river and not to give them away, though a lame man and a drowning man will plead for her help. The pennies are for her soul and must not be given away.

Psyche does as she is told and is almost safely back when curiosity causes her to open the box. Immediately she is overcome with sleep. Her husband Eros senses her danger and wakens her. He brings her to the gods and she is declared worthy to be a goddess. (In one version, the veil of virginity is given back to her.) The child born to them is named Pleasure.

There is so much rich symbolism in this story. It shows how distrust and envy endangers relationships. Consciousness— light—must be brought into the most paradisal relationships, whatever the wounding that may result.

How terrified I was when in my twenties my relationship to God was illumined by consciousness of my own hidden and often unworthy motives for entering the convent. How all light and pleasure seemed to fall from my calling. In what despair I was.

Totally removed seemed those previous moments in the novitiate when I knelt in adoration, memorizing the psalm, "My God, I have watched for you from the break of dawn." Or the moment

of putting on the beautiful long white twelfth-century habit, feeling I would indeed with all my heart try to be a stainless bride—
"Receive, Sister, this veil, which may you preserve stainless before
the tribunal of our Lord Jesus Christ," the priest had prayed over
me. All had seemed possible and comforting.

But with the knife of discrimination and the light of fuller consciousness all affective connection to this ideal seemed to have fled.
I felt I was in despair. I can understand why Psyche wanted to
throw herself into the river. I threw myself into the river of work. I
threw away romantic notions of religious life or of marriage—
"Those are adolescent dreams," I thought; I smiled at the romantic fervor of young novices: "They'll learn." I smiled.

I am sure that every woman and man is called to embrace, to
live through, such a disillusionment. I am sure, too, that each of
us is called, like Psyche, to start on the long, hard road of reap-
propriation, of finding the fullness of love in fullness of consciousness the second time around.

Love is better the second time around, but only, I think, because of the courageous completion of the four tasks that enable
us in the end, like Psyche, to be awakened by love. Many, I know,
and you know too, who never go down that long lonesome road
back to Eros. Erich Fromm, in his classic *Art of Loving,* thinks that
most give up the task of becoming true lovers and drown in work.
Perhaps this is another exemplification of Jesus' saying, "Many
are called, but few are chosen." It is important for you to reflect if
you have ignored the call to reappropriate the fullness of love in
your life after the wounding and loss of first love.

I see myself right now inwardly struggling with Psyche's tasks,
sometimes in order, sometimes all at once. The sorting of seeds is
for me the task of choosing from a deep feminine priority what are
the tasks that will keep me in Eros, in relation to myself, to others,
and to God.

So many tasks pluck at me—thousands of incipient seeds, all
good, waiting for me, Johnny Appleseed, to do the broadcasting.
Sorting takes infinite patience and the primitive instinct of ants,
who are practical and close to the earth. When I am flying in the
air I imagine that I can do all—be all things—but my "ants"
know that I can only do one thing at a time well. Pursuing a life of

love demands rigorous and patient sorting. (Fromm suggests that a true lover ruthlessly refrains from trivial conversation, for instance.)

This sorting seems most difficult for women. We are used to letting our collective role as nun or mother (helper, nurturer) set out our tasks. How can we say "no" to so many reaching hands? But sorting, too, is a courageous act. If I fail to sort, I give away my time, my talent, and sometimes, my soul. I spill myself thoughtlessly to the world, and weep that it bears so little fruit. (What sorting do you find hard? When do you spill yourself out senselessly?)

The second task reminds me that love (relatedness) requires that I need not fight head-on. It is a waste of my life and energy to ram into people and things. I don't have to fight for everything. I can take leftovers, and that can suffice.

It is ironic to me that as a shy, gentle, introverted girl I had to learn to become more aggressive, more willing to speak out, to stand and fight. But the water reed reminds me as the Taoists teach, that water which flows around things is, in the end more powerful than earth, air, and fire. It can be slapped, channeled, poured out or into any shape, but it carves canyons through powerful stone.

The feminine principle is a flowing one and I am struggling to learn watery ways. In depth relations, head-on assaults are counterproductive; we are all too vulnerable. Lowered expectations, the empty water reed, and twilight harvesting pave the way to Eros.

The third task reminds me of how fragile is the vase—this body—in which I carry my small portion of the powerful waters of life. How I need the perspective of the eagle to take the long view—to keep me humble and grounded before the torrent from which I drink. We carry our treasure, says St. Paul, in earthen vessels—easily broken. For Psyche, the vessel is crystal—an image of the transparency to ourselves and others and God that enables us to love deeply, to drink deeply from both the beauty and pain of life. When you have felt yourself earthbound, who or what has been an "eagle" to help you gain perspective?

The last task (one that Robert Johnson in *She* thinks that few souls accomplish) is the trip down back to the underworld for the sake of inner beauty. Carl Jung has said that men (and women) will do anything, no matter how absurd, to avoid facing their souls. They are terrified to face their inner world with its ambiguity and chaos.

The myth suggests that when a woman goes down into the depth of her soul, the last temptation is her inability to say "no"; to close the open hand. We women are so trained to give, that sometimes we give away our soul penny, unable to return to fully autonomous consciousness. Our maternal instinct, our pity for the lame and drowning, blinds us to our own soul's cry; and we abandon the quest for depth.

This is a delicate discernment, when love of neighbor requires that we first heal ourselves, as good physicians. The myth reminds me that our deep soul work demands some of our prime energy, our inner and outer money. How difficult it is to say a creative "no"—how conditioned we are to think that a "yes" is always creative. When have you given away a soul penny, when have you said "yes" when a deeper obedience required a "no"?

The last temptation/trial of Psyche concerns curiosity. Bernard of Clairvaux considers curiosity one of the most serious obstacles to the inner life. If we keep poking and looking about inside ourselves, God's work is somehow violated—the seed must be watered, but left embedded in its soil. We must do all we can, and then wait in darkness—"Teach us to care and not to care," T. S. Eliot writes; to watch and yet not watch.

I am in a way, however, comforted that Psyche, courageous through all her pain and trials, is not so perfect in the end—that she falters—that foolishly, womanly, she wanted to see the secret of beauty. Surely it must have been the combination of her courage and frailty that drew Eros near to her again, to awaken her with his love.

How lovely the thought of being awakened by love! How close to the Christian notion of grace. We do all that we can and yet we do not *earn* what we receive. It is a gift awakening us to a divine world—far beyond what our efforts in the underworld could purchase. That is the hope of each Christian as her eyes close in sleep, wearied by life's trials, haunted by the hope of lasting beauty;

that on the other side we will be awakened by love: "And there stood Jesus standing on the shore" (John 21:4).

The child Psyche bears is named "pleasure" or joy. So few of us hard-working Christians bear this fruit. Yet we know that it is the vital sign of sanctity. And maybe we don't awaken to joy because we don't let sorrow carve deeply into our being as Gibran says. We do not track down our despairs, ask for help, honor their tasks as Psyche did. Every book we read, every relationship we struggle with, every technique we embrace should be for the greater enjoyment of God.

I have on the wall of my bedroom a Christmas card received twenty-nine years ago, with one word on it—Joy. For the first five years in religious life, in the Pentecost drawing of holy cards, mine always read, "Joy." This I know and trust—this is the promise I follow, the good news of joy.

Christ means to me that pain is no dead end! We have helpers all about and grace poured out, pressed down, running over. We have love pursuing us, even as we think we pursue him. We were born God's imagination creating a gift for the world, meant to pass from sorrow to joy; to be awakened to joy by love himself.

Your Response
What does the myth of Amor and Psyche mean to you? Here are some questions:

1. When, in your life relationships, have you consciously or unconsciously brought a knife and lamp that changed the paradisal darkness? Did your love flee, never to be found again, or only for a time?

2. When, if ever, have you experienced that "Love is better the second time around"?

3. Do you have difficulty "sorting the seeds" of your life?

4. Do you have difficulty gathering the ram's fleece at night? Do you tend to fight head on? Do you really believe that water is the most powerful of elements; that flowing is better than burning?

5. When you have felt yourself earthbound, who or what has been an eagle to help you gain perspective?

6. When have you given away a soul penny, when have you said "yes" when a deeper obedience required a "no"?

7. When have you been awakened by love?

8. What have been the most joyful moments of your life? Do you practice joy? Or do you consider it a mood passively received?

Response to Amor and Psyche

RONDA CHERVIN

I love the feeling of hope-for-the-journey conveyed in Mary Neill's commentary on this myth, rather unfamiliar to me.

I find it hard to respond because I think of myself as a lover and yet I find that I have failed often in the courageous tasks of the love Mary outlines.

In answer to her questions:

I *always* escape into work to avoid the pain of love. Also, I try vainly to flee from the cross of love into some nirvana of religious bliss. Only after many denials on God's part am I willing to see that he is part of the pain, that he will not tranquilize me because he wants to bring out the greatest inner beauty and compassion for others out of the pain of love he has permitted for me as part of the script for my Woman's Tale.

Very insightful for me was Mary's idea of sorting out seeds of love patiently vs. spilling out all over. Saying creative "no's" has always seemed impossible for me. I trade in the peace of soul the Lord wants for me for the possibility of a tiny ounce of admiration—the busy commitments often making me too tied up for the daily back and forth of friendship love.

The image of seeking inner buried beauty without losing one's identity is also very evocative. It probably explains the terror of mysticism so many experience. We say we want to "go all the way" in response to God's love but we are terrified of the dark abysses within. It seems that opening the door to the inner self necessarily means confronting demonic forces or making oneself so vulnerable that one would surrender to any strong force. During long periods of inwardness I begin to understand how important practical mundane tasks are to keep one sane. And yet at the end of such bouts with the unconscious, there is new beauty.

Joy coming after failure is such an interesting category. Often it comes through some minor part of life being unexpectedly refreshing, such as the charm of the playground, the beauty of a dog, the fun of knitting or ice-skating, the sudden sound of a favorite piece of music on the radio. God's equivalent of a "nice bowl of Jewish chicken soup"!

Sometimes joy comes in unexpected graces when God seems to lightly brush away the tears and then it seems that failure is nothing and LOVE everything—an everything so powerful that the blocking of any human source is as nothing.

Part 3

MY WOMAN'S TALE

The time has come to crystallize our journey into a final image or statement. Read those written by Mary and Ronda and then write your own, in the form of prose, a poem, your own fairytale.

⚜ My Woman's Tale
And They Lived Happily Ever After

MARY NEILL

Be like your heavenly mother Mary, and you'll be a woman," I heard, and maybe that's exactly what they said. Wrapped in smallness and fear, I could draw strength from that towering Mother of us all, Mater dolorosa in whom the Word became struggling flesh. I know the recipe for Mater dolorosa bread quite well:

Take one woman, knead her well with searching, pleading, needing, losing, fading—bake her into a thin passover bread—eaten with bitter herbs standing in the desert, salted with her tears, sandwiched between Egypt, whose leeks and cucumbers she must not regret, and the promised land whose milk and honey never may touch her lips.

Split her into Snow White/Rose Red; freeze her into Briar Rose asleep; dance her to death in red shoes; lock her Rapunzel-high in towers cursed by parents' sin; give her ashes to eat on Cinderella's hearth; let wolves devour her in her mother's mother's home; let ugly beasts pursue her heart and hand; leave her standing wounded to the core, deserted by Goethe, Gynt, or Kierke-gaard—by everyman; let her psyche, her soul, sob before the million seeds to sort, the ram, the crag, the entombing underworld. Take one woman, any woman, every woman, bake her well and long in the oven of sadness until her heart burns red-brown.

But if woman's task fate is not only baking, but sewing, how do you clothe such a woman in a garment of joy? Where find the thread? The pattern, the spindle? Then when to cut and where to sew? If the Gospel had been written by a woman, she would, perhaps, have woven more brightness into that somber landscape—not only thunderbolts upon a hill of pain.

Were I reweaving Mary's story there, I would indeed weave in the part about the seven swords that pierced her heart in somber tones: "Be it done to me according to your word," she said, saying yes to life and to a darkened reputation. If Joseph did not understand, why should the neighbors? "And the Word was made flesh."

"I must be about my Father's business," he replies to her anxious search through three darkened days, lost on the road from the city on the hill. "And the Word was made loss."

"Woman, my hour is not come," her Son replies, but she must press him until he presses water into wine. "And the Word was made wine."

"Your mother and your brothers are outside seeking you," he is told, and his "Who is my mother?" must have thudded sharp against her ever-searching soul. "Òi vey, such a strange son," her Jewish neighbors said and her Jewish heart agreed. "And the Word was made confusion."

And then it comes to this that she must stand before the shameful cross, take him dead into her arms to clean, to hold but briefly and place him in a darkened tomb. "And the Word was made death."

And she must hear from others, from a fallen woman Magdalene, a faltering disciple Peter, a rabid teenaged John that her only flesh, her son had come again and gone, calling them to move again, and yet again to Galilee and then beyond. "And the Word was made transfigured flesh that faded from one's touch."

What sadness plagued this Mary's life and ours—mater, femina, mulier, dolorosa—crying, calling, weeping, searching, needing, losing, birthing, finding—only to lose again, and yet again.

But if as I said I were rewriting the Gospel, I'd warp in more of the joys, however small, and illuminate them carefully, like Jesus' woman friend who spent the night searching out one small coin.

Letting go of sadness takes heavy courage too and special movements of the heart and so must it have been for that Mother of us all. They never tell the seven joys of Mary; just about the seven swords that pierced her heart.

So I'll weave them through for you, and for me: the "yes" that causes heart and womb to jerk with joy; the gifts that come in dark birthing cave, the gifts that one could never plan upon—not just gold and ointment, but perfume!; the Joseph that loves you even if he does not understand himself, or you; the eyes born from you and colored by your own which suddenly mirror a new world back to you (a world where no is also yes); the friends that stand beside you in the agony of death—who do not care if your son, or even you yourself—are criminal; the stranger who lends you a tomb for your dead child, and your deadened heart; the gifts of fire that stream from heaven onto a clot of cowards locked away for fear in the small comfort of an upper room.

And maybe there is even an eighth joy, too; for seven is a man's number, lean and uneven; eight is feminine—two even circles closed against the storm. The joy, whether sharply known or dimly felt that your pain was just an antiphon to joy—not the total somber psalm of life.

They teach about the pain, those holy, heavy books, and maybe they descry the joy, but it was not there, I think, that I learned to harvest joy: where to find, scythe, weigh it, press it down until it runs over the brim. But this has been the gift of fairytales to me—of my own silly story. To learn the roads to joy so clearly patterned there—mothering all our snow-white, rose-red opposites, letting frozen beauty come to life; risking confirmation in our frenzied dance; not lingering long in wayside homes; letting down our golden hair to wandering love; dancing until the dawn in shoes that shatter; picking flowers on the way to rendezvous; kissing ugliness within and out; naming "desertion" "emptied for more life," instead of "death"; learning to be awakened by love. "And the Word was made joy."

Frail sister Joy, squeezed between our woes.
Whoever thought you strong enough to bear our pain?
Whoever could have seen you hidden in the seeds of discontent?

Who could have known that you were to come like honey—thick
  and nourishing, condensed from a thousand winged trips of banal bees?
Not me—I never knew it.
I once was baked in sadness, and now I am wearing joy.
I've known sad saints and happy saints; sad endings and happy endings,
  tragedies and fairy tales. I've known sadness and joy. "Joy is better"
I want to say—shutting out my sister sadness. But I have learned.
They are both my sisters. Womanlike I bake and weave. "And your joy no
  one shall take from you."
"And they lived happily ever after."

⚜ My Woman's Tale

RONDA CHERVIN

A family occurrence provides me with my deepest image of my own womanhood. One of my children was in pain. During the night she crawled into bed between myself and my husband. As I lay awake listening to the sound of her breathing I felt her pain right inside myself, my husband's strength around us all, and God's Fatherly love enclosing us in his embrace.

I thought: to be a woman for me is to be held, to receive new life, to give birth to babies, to books, to new courses; and then to love them and hold them and give to them of my substance.

Perhaps this image will seem traditional to some readers. For me it is a breakthrough to become convinced that such a primordial image is intrinsic to my own happiness. To realize that I am not happy when I strive to be strong out of my own strength, creative by flight from involvement with others, denying my own neediness. My happiness is to let God himself or through others hold me still to give me love and truth and beauty, and then to let this overflow to others.

For me then, to be a woman is to trust in love and to be faithful to the call of love amidst all difficulties.

Working with Mary Neill has helped me to see my life not so much as a series of failures and successes but more like a tale with episodes full of buried treasures, sure to have a happy ending if only I persevere.

Working on the entries in the book shows me a picture of a cycle from sheltered "little Ronda" going out into the world with her gift, to rejection, fear, crusading, failure, despair, search for human idols to be dependent on, return to littleness in the arms of

God, and then going out with the true gift to those I am given to love and receive love from . . . and then the cycle repeats? Necessarily? As painfully? Maybe not! In fact, writing this book has exorcized many of my inner demons.

Do the powerful symbols of the fairytale women contain messages for me about what it is like to be possessed by a tragic destiny and what it is to be liberated? Yes.

Snow-White and Rose-Red can fight all day or they can love each other.

The Red Shoes can dance me to death or let me leap into new forms of creativity—if only I trust enough in love to dance more slowly.

I can become bitter when I don't fit into the chairs in the house of the bears, or I can accept life as a pilgrimage—if only I trust that God has a part in writing my tale.

If I trust in the strength of love instead of loving the strength of force perhaps I will learn how to *point* the scarecrows, the tin woodmen, and the cowardly lions down the yellow brick road instead of *shoving* them down it!

If I learn to trust enough in the power of love to transform the domestic tasks of family life I might not have to flee to fantasy balls, for ordinary life itself would be more of a ball.

If I believe in Christ, my God who suffered and died out of love, I might have the courage to weep in the thorn-bush like Rapunzel and then to open the eyes of the blind with my tears.

Wouldn't my sense of failure and despair be less if I refused to let myself be a victim of witches or a prey to wolves? Healed of self-hatred I would not be so eager to be punished by the barbs of the envious or to annihilate myself as a supper for wolves! With greater self-love I would become the victorious sister Gretel and the Red Riding Hood who comes out whole even from deadly encounters!

If I trusted in love I would become like Beauty, able to kiss beasts until their princely nature is revealed—even to kiss the beastliness that is sometimes inherent in life itself.

Letting Christ heal me of desertion I will cease to look for idols to worship and then fired by the Spirit I can go out courageously to do the tasks of love.

In the midst of my own intense struggle with the destructive and creative forces in my own selfhood I feel a deep identity with all my sisters. I sense your sufferings, despair, and hope as you spin your tales. This book has been my way of weeping and rejoicing with you.

Because for me the most profound source of hope is a religious vision I have to add here for you one last image of womanliness coming from God. I see the saints as the women most willing to let God write the tale of their lives and I take hope from seeing the wild passion of Mary Magdalene turned into holy love by the kiss of Jesus. I take courage from the thought of the crusading Joan of Arc winning and lossing battles through total submission to a supernatural vision. I laugh to think that Martha the frantic housewife grew into sanctity . . . and I see all these feminine archetypes fulfilled in the image of the Virgin Mother Mary—her Jewish heart totally open in surrender to God the Father, wedded by the Spirit, giving birth to the Divine Child, pierced by suffering in compassionate empathy for all of us, finally to be crowned in the heaven of the eternal kingdom where love alone will reign.

Rereading the original questions of *The Woman's Tale* I think I can honestly reply now after this stage of the journey is completed.

What do I hate about being a woman? Nothing.

What do I love about being a woman? Everything.

What does being a woman cost? Everything.

Is it worth it? Yes!

Now is the time for you to reread your notebook and write a final entry entitled: My Woman's Tale by ⸻

Notes

1 *Thomas Merton, Monk,* ed. Patrick Hart (New York: Image Books, 1976), p. 14.
2 Bettelheim, Bruno, *The Uses of Enchantment* (New York: Knopf, 1976), p. 217.
3 For a description of the path leading to my conversion see the After-word of my book *Church of Love* (Liguori, Mo.: Liguori Publications, 1972). For my reasonings affirming Catholic ethics see *Christian Ethics and Your Everyday Life* (Los Angeles: S.C.R.C. Publications, 1979).
4 Jung, Carl G., *Psychological Reflections* (New York: Harper Torchbooks, Harper and Brothers, 1961), p. 89.

Suggestions for Further Reading

Both authors have contributed to this list of books. (Ronda Chervin's contributions will be identified by *, Mary Neill's by †.) Some entries refer to specific works, others to the works in general of a specific author.

Anscombe, Elizabeth, the most influential British analytic woman philosopher. Anscombe edited and helped write *Nuclear Weapons: A Catholic Response* (New York: Sheed and Ward, 1962) which contains some of the best attacks on nuclear weapons. For a defense of the church's position against artificial contraception see *Contraception and Chastity*, Catholic Truth Society, 1975.*

Back, G. R., *The Intimate Enemy.* New York: William Morrow, 1969. Very helpful for those who never learned the importance of fighting and the proper skills as participant or observer when intimates fight. A helpful "how-to" book.†

Beauvoir, Simone de, Although I disagree with almost all this famous French philosopher's premises, I find her writing on all topics fascinating and stimulating. The most comprehensive of her works on woman is *The Second Sex* (New York: Knopf, 1971). Perceptive portraits of women of all classes can be found in her novels and short stories. I find these even more interesting than her nonfiction works.*

Becker, Ernest, *The Denial of Death.* New York: Free Press, 1973. This is one of the few books that scared me when I read it. Invaluable for understanding the problems of morality as those of changing "hero systems." A sociologist, Becker seeks to prove that evidence from clinical psychology supports insights about human nature that religionists have always held. He leans heavily on Rank and Kierkegaard.†

Bettelheim, Bruno, *The Uses of Enchantment.* New York: Knopf, 1976. A solidly Freudian interpretation of fairytales, well researched with some helpful insights. Sometimes heavy going if you are easily bored by a tendency to positivistic, reductionist interpretations.†

Bonhoeffer, Dietrich, *The Cost of Discipleship*. New York: Macmillan, 1964. The name says it. A good reminder for "bargain hunters." Fine for meditation.†

Friday, Nancy, *My Mother, My Self.* New York: Dell, 1979. Don't be put off by the popularity of this book and Friday's willingness to disclose what most of use would never utter. She asks all the right questions, or most of them, and even your irritation in reading her leads to fruitful insights. She is honest.†

Harding, M. Esther, *The Way of All Women*. New York: Harper Colophon, 1975. This is a "classic" Jungian understanding of feminine development, offering helpful insights for those working through their resistance to being an ornament to someone else's life.†

Hart, Patrick, ed. *Thomas Merton, Monk*. New York: Image Books, 1976. Merton has been for me and for many a mentor in combining twentieth-century consciousness and deep spirituality. This is a good introduction to Merton the man, as seen by those who lived with him, and those who knew him well.†

Haughton, Rosemary, *Tales from Eternity*. New York: Seabury Press, 1973. A well-wrought reflection on the spiritual depth contained in fairytales.†

Hildebrand, Dietrich and Alice von, I highly recommend the books of these two Catholic philosophers. The most accessible to the nonscholarly reader are *Man and Woman* (Chicago: Franciscan Herald Press, 1966) and *The Art of Living*, by the same publisher.*

Jaffe, Aniele, ed. C. G. Jung, *Psychological Reflections*. New York: Harper & Row, 1971. This is a good collection of some of Jung's sayings, fine for meditation.†

Johnson, Robert A., *She*. Harper & Row, 1977. A fine explication of the Amor and Psyche myth, with helpful insights for spiritual growth in a feminine way.†

Jung, Carl, *Man and His Symbols*. Dell, 1978. Again, though you may not agree with all of Jung's solutions, he asks some very important questions and gives very fruitful insights about the journey of the soul.†

Kierkegaard, Sören, *The Works of Love*. Harper & Row, 1964. Beautiful reflections on each of the New Testament texts that speak of love.*†

Layard, John, *The Virgin Archetype*. New York: Spring Publications, 1972. Gives a helpful understanding of the meaning of virginity, its relation to marriage and to spiritual development. Transformation of energy is the name of the game, whether one is celibate or married.†

Le Fort, Gertrud von, A German novelist and thinker of a forceful dramatic and mystical bent. Her book *The Eternal Woman* will inspire the reader's imagination.*

Lewis, C. S., *Till We Have Faces*. Grand Rapids, Mich.: Wm. Eerdmans Publishing Co., 1956. A powerfully written novel based on the Amor and Psyche story, as perceived by the ugly sister.*†

Maritain, Raissa, Another Frenchwoman. She was a Jewish convert to the Catholic church, and the wife and intellectual companion of Jacques Maritain. Of all her writings, I find the one published by her husband after her death, *Raissa's Journal,* to be the most poignant.*

Merton, Thomas, and Griffith, J. H., *A Hidden Wholeness*. Boston: Houghton Mifflin Co., 1970. Looking at pictures of Merton and photographs taken by him concretizes his spirituality in a new way for me. This was compiled and written about after his death by his close friend Griffith (author of *Black Like Me*).†

Murdoch, Iris, A witty and challenging contemporary English novelist. Her writings focus on the many amusing ways modern men and women find to make sophisticated excuses for unloving behavior. The essence of her life view can be found in a small philosophical work entitled *The Sovereignty of the Good* (New York: Schocken Books, 1970). It will surprise you if you interpret Murdoch as a supporter of the hedonism of her characters.*

Neuman, Erich, *Amor and Psyche*. Princeton, New Jersey: Princeton University Press, 1971. Another insightful interpretation of the journey of the feminine by a Jungian. More scholarly than Johnson's.†

O'Connor, Flannery, Recently I have gone on an O'Connor binge. The haunting prophetic novels of this Southern Catholic writer such as *Wise Blood* and *The Violent Bear It Away* highlight the importance of total commitment. A recent collection of her letters entitled *The Habit of Being* contains beautifully concise formulations of theological truth as well as a glimpse of her own very humorous personality. All her works are published by Farrar, Straus, and Giroux in New York City.*

Sanford, John, *Healing and Wholeness*. New York City: Paulist Press, 1977. A very helpful and practical explication by a Jungian.†

Speyr, Adrienne von, The works of this brilliant theologian are slowly being translated into English. She combines clarity of expression with great depth of insight. Her classic is about Mary and is called *The Handmaid of the Lord* (London: Harvill, 1956). Also translated is a remarkable work on penance called *Confession* (New York: Herder & Herder, 1965) very contemporary in its emphasis on personal conversion. Alba House has published a book on vocation called *They Followed His Call* (1979).†

Stein, Edith, A Jewish phenomenologist who became first a Catholic and then a Carmelite nun, finally to be incinerated in a Nazi concentration camp. Edith Stein wrote several books about philosophical topics. The writing most interesting for our topics is on the Education of Woman, in which she delineates different types of feminine personality. A book of her *Writings* was published by Peter Owen in London, in 1956.*

Stern, Karl, This contemporary psychiatrist's account of the nature of woman in *The Flight from Woman* (New York: Noonday, 1969) defends the theory that the male psyche is truncated because of its rejection of the feminine. He traces the psychosis of the antifeminine back through the writings of male philosophers and literary men.*

Ulanov, Ann Belford, *The Feminine*. Evanston, Ill.: Northwestern University Press, 1971. A scholarly and comprehensive effort to unite Jungian theory about the feminine with theology.†

Undset, Sigrid, I believe that this Norwegian Nobel Prize-winning novelist is the best woman writer of all times. For years I refrained from reading her because of the formidable titles of her historical novels. Although set in medieval times the themes are thoroughly modern. The most famous are *Kristen Lavransdatter* and *The Master of Hestviken*. Both are now available in paperback (*Kristen* by Bantam, 1978, and *Hestviken* by NAL, 1978).*

Since the issue of feminism has come into prominence I have spent most of my leisure time rereading novelists such as George Eliot and Jane Austen, poets such as Emily Dickinson, and the lives of the women saints. It is well worth mining the past to discover how heroic and brilliant women have been. I recommend that all our readers dip into these works for new sources of strength.*